PURPOSEFUL
Writing Assessment

PURPOSEFUL
Writing Assessment

Using Multiple-Choice Practice to Inform Writing Instruction

Susan Koehler

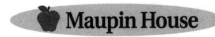

Purposeful Writing Assessment
Using Multiple-choice Practice to Inform Writing Instruction

Cover, book design, and layout: Candace Hollinger

Library of Congress Cataloging-in-Publication Data

Koehler, Susan, 1963-

  Purposeful writing assessment : using multiple-choice practice to inform writing instruction / Susan Koehler.

   p. cm.

  Includes bibliographical references and index.

  ISBN-13: 978-1-934338-18-6 (pbk.)

  ISBN-10: 1-934338-18-4 (pbk.)

  1. English language--Composition and exercises--Study and teaching (Elementary) 2. English language--Composition and exercises--Ability testing. 3. Lesson planning. I. Title.

  LB1576.K564 2008

  372.62'3044--dc22

2008016234

ISBN-13: 978-1-934338-18-6

Maupin House publishes professional resources for K-12 educators. Contact us for tailored, in-school training or to schedule an author for a workshop or conference.
Visit www.maupinhouse.com for free lesson plan downloads.

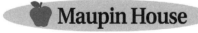

Maupin House Publishing, Inc.
2416 NW 71 Place
Gainesville, FL 32653
www.maupinhouse.com
800-524-0634
352-373-5588
352-373-5546 (fax)
info@maupinhouse.com

10 9 8 7 6 5 4 3 2 1

Table of Contents

Introduction

Purposeful Assessment

In the world of high-stakes testing, the word "assessment" has become practically synonymous with the concept of accountability. Purposeful assessment, however, is a powerful concept that wise educators use to inform their instruction.

When used as a diagnostic tool, assessments produce much more than a number that can be applied to assess how well a student is functioning. They provide a window into a student's patterns of thinking and processing information. Once these patterns are discovered, teaching and re-teaching can be targeted and differentiated to respond to and address the weaknesses for maximum effectiveness.

Writing Assessment

Like reading and math, writing assessment is now required in most states. Unlike math with its clearly right and wrong answers, however, writing by its very nature opens itself to subjective scoring. Because of that, test developers have worked to standardize scoring procedures. The result is a tendency toward holistic rubric scoring and the emergence of the multiple-choice writing assessment.

Of course, holistic rubrics can be effective in scoring a student's writing. With extensive training and practice, scorers can be quite consistent in assigning scores to written pieces. However, an element of subjectivity almost always exists. Therefore, many states have amended writing assessment to include multiple-choice formats.

Multiple-choice writing assessments tend to evaluate a student's knowledge of skills in three major areas of the writing process:

- focus and organization
- style and composition
- conventions and mechanics

Within these three broad categories, individual skills are identified and tested. When multiple-choice tests are viewed as simple tools for scoring competency, much of their real value is lost. If, on the other hand, multiple-choice tests are viewed as tools for instructional planning, the tests become a quick and efficient way to identify areas of focus for subsequent instruction. This book will show you exactly how to use multiple-choice practice to inform your writing instruction.

Focus and Organization

Focus and organization skills include the gathering of pertinent information, planning, and organizing information for effective communication. In a well-organized piece, the details are all relevant to a clearly identifiable topic. The piece begins with an inviting introduction, is well-paced and focused, and ends with a satisfying conclusion.

The well-organized piece is easy to follow. Main ideas stand out, concrete details support the main ideas, and transitions are present to connect ideas and assist the reader in following the writer's logical flow of information. The purpose and audience, while not explicitly identified, are appropriate to the situation and consistent throughout the piece.

Style and Composition

Style and composition are the elements that bring interest and enjoyment to the reader. Sentence variation, description, figurative language, voice, and word choice are carefully crafted to be precise and engaging.

In written pieces, these craft skills demonstrate a sense of maturity and achievement. Young writers should be explicitly taught to use style and composition skills and should refer to these skills as they revise written pieces for clarity and interest.

Mechanics and Conventions

When used properly, spelling, punctuation, grammar, and usage skills are hardly noticed; however, errors in language conventions distract and confuse the reader. Students should be taught to self-correct errors in mechanics and conventions during the editing phase of the writing process.

Most essay assessments allow some flexibility in the application of language conventions, but common expectations are for students to:

- spell frequently used words appropriately
- make close approximations of more difficult words
- demonstrate subject-verb agreement
- demonstrate noun-pronoun agreement
- use capitalization where needed
- use basic punctuation correctly (end marks, commas in a series, quotation marks)

Multiple-choice writing assessments usually require students to identify errors, or ask them to identify the one correctly written phrase or sentence in a group.

How to Use This Book

This book is designed to give teachers convenient tools for conducting purposeful writing assessment based on multiple-choice practice. The two separate assessments provided for each skill set will give you valuable information that will guide instruction and monitor progress.

Appendix A contains the Comprehensive Writing Assessments, Form A and Form B. The Form A assessment is designed to be given first. Incorrect responses should be analyzed to determine error patterns and misconceptions. This can be given at the beginning of the year as a pre-test, to gain insight into your students' background knowledge about writing so that you can design your curriculum to meet their specific needs. Or, you can give it during the year as you begin a new writing unit.

After re-teaching and practice have occurred, give the Form B assessment to determine the effectiveness of re-teaching and to ensure that the student has mastered the specific skill. This can happen at the end of a unit or at the end of the school year to assess growth and achievement as a post-test.

An answer key and a list of re-teaching strategies are provided for each skill set. Master lists of professional books that address each skill set and literature models to help teach specific skills are also included in the Resources.

Nurturing Young Writers

While multiple-choice practice is an efficient way to assess students' knowledge of the skills involved in writing and gain familiarity with a multiple-choice format, these assessments should never become stand-alone instruction. Students must understand how to apply what they know as they write original compositions. You will find this book to be a valuable supplemental tool that you can use before and after you explicitly teach writing-craft skills.

Be sure to allow time daily for students to write in a workshop atmosphere. Identifying skills and applying skills are different processes, and students should have ample opportunities for each.

Much of the writing that students are required to complete in schools is prompted, but it is important to allow for self-selected topics as well. Motivation and engagement are generally higher when students write about topics of personal choice. This continuous writing practice also serves as an ongoing, formative assessment that complements work with this book. Maintain a balance of limited timed, writing-upon-demand situations and ample open-ended, self-selected topics.

The Reading-Writing Connection

The reciprocal processes of reading and writing can and should be used to complement and support each other. Use literature models abundantly to demonstrate the effective application of writing-craft skills. Encourage students to find examples of skills that demonstrate organization and focus, style and composition, and conventions and mechanics.

Discuss the impact and strength of word choice and figurative language as used by published authors. When students learn how to analyze literature and identify craft, their ability to apply craft to their own written compositions is strengthened.

Preparing Students for Standardized Writing Assessments

These multiple-choice assessments are designed to assess a student's knowledge of the skills that add focus, organization, style, and accuracy to a student's writing. There is a difference between being able to identify and generate these skills. Simply recognizing these skills does not imply that the student will be able to create pieces with original word choice, descriptive language, and varied, engaging sentence structure.

However, if students are unable to recognize these skills, it is highly unlikely that they will be able to produce them in original compositions. This makes diagnosis an important *starting* point. You must be sure to carry these skills to the next level by modeling their use in literary works and providing ample practice for students to create lively, engaging text.

While the primary purpose of these assessments is for meaningful writing instruction, they also provide practice in applying test-taking strategies and preparing for standardized, multiple-choice assessments. These skills are significant not only to the evaluation of a student's knowledge of skills related to writing, but also to the evaluation of a student's reading comprehension and facility with literary skills.

Keep in mind that test-taking strategies can be explicitly taught to help students demonstrate their true proficiency with writing skills when being evaluated with multiple-choice assessments. Teach students to read questions carefully, to understand what's being asked before reading answer choices, and to read all answer choices before selecting a response.

The Big Picture

While the explicit teaching of specific writing skills is essential for student achievement, mastery of individual skills is really not the ultimate goal of writing instruction.

Achievement of these skills is a step toward our ultimate goal in the teaching of writing: to produce students who can think critically, comprehend written language, and communicate effectively through writing. Assessment, used purposefully, can be a powerful component in achieving these goals.

Chapter One
Organization and Focus

Organizational skills are taught in all major writing curricula because thoughtful organization is essential to effective written communication. Methods and styles vary, but organization generally involves four parts:

- gathering data
- planning
- beginning, middle, and end
- maintaining focus

Different genres require different types of organization, and these differences should be addressed during instruction. Narrative writing—whether fictional or personal narrative—is rooted in chronological order, so planning schemes should be linear, such as time lines and ordered lists of events.

Expository writing is well-suited for outlines and webs, because its organization is based on the sorting and grouping of related details. The only exception to this rule is procedural or how-to writing, which should be organized linearly.

Evaluating Organizational Skills

Weak organizational skills stand out immediately to a reader. Stories that are difficult to follow, pieces that leave the reader without a clear sense of focus or resolution, and expository pieces that lack adequate support are all signs of deficient organizational skills.

Multiple-choice assessments are useful to diagnose the precise areas of difficulty. Once the areas of difficulty are identified, they can be addressed with re-teaching and practice. Follow-up assessment is then useful in evaluating the effectiveness of the strategies employed.

Assessments

In this section, you will find two kinds of multiple-choice organizational assessments. The first type mainly addresses data collection and planning. Planning schemes are presented in genre-specific formats, and students are asked to select responses that will give the teacher information about how well the student is able to identify good and poor planning strategies, as well as beginnings and endings of written pieces.

The second type of assessment presents a written draft and requires students to analyze elements of focus, support, beginnings and endings. All of these assessments can be quickly administered and scored, so that targeted re-teaching can begin immediately. Answer keys are embedded in each assessment and all assessments have ten questions for easy scoring if grades are being assigned.

Assessments 1-5 are tailored to address the following specific genres:

- personal narrative
- fictional narrative
- expository

Re-teaching and Re-testing

Each assessment contains two tests, Form A and Form B. The specific questions and answer choices are different, but the types of items presented are the same. Form A should be administered as a diagnostic tool. Once scored, the teacher can identify specific error patterns and target instruction for those skills identified.

Following Form A, you will find an answer key for convenient scoring and a list of suggestions for re-teaching. These suggestions are genre-specific and tailored to cover typical error patterns. For further information and reading that can yield additional strategies, a brief bibliography of professional books and a cross-index of literature models are supplied in the Resources.

After re-teaching and practice, administer Form B. This second assessment will indicate the effectiveness of the strategies employed. Of course, if a student's performance is flawless on Form A, there is no need for re-teaching and administration of Form B.

Assessments – Organization Skills

Assessment 1: Planning for a personal narrative piece

Form A

Form B

Assessment 2: Planning for a fictional narrative piece

Form A

Form B

Assessment 3: Planning for an expository piece

Form A

Form B

Assessment 4: Analyzing a narrative piece

Form A

Form B

Assessment 5: Analyzing an expository piece

Form A

Form B

> *Everyone has had an embarrassing experience. Think about a time when you felt embarrassed. Write to tell about your embarrassing experience.*

Jonah's teacher gave this prompt to him and Jonah created the following plan:

7:00	Woke up and ate breakfast.
7:30	Got dressed, brushed teeth, walked to bus stop.
8:00	Arrived at bus stop a little late, afraid I missed bus.
8:01	Bus came. No one there but sleeping kid in back.
8:05	Next stop: "New kids" got on bus.
8:08	Next stop: More kids I didn't recognize.
8:12	Realized other kids were older – bus was for middle school.

8:13	Slumped in seat. Pretended to be asleep. Tried to think of plan. Possible plans:
	    Get off at middle school.
	    Tell bus driver I'm on wrong bus.
	    Stay on bus and see where it goes next.

8:25	Arrived at middle school. Talked to driver. Driver laughed and took me to my school.
8:40	Arrived at school late. Driver explained to principal.
3:00	School was out, everyone knew. They kept pointing out my bus to go home.

1. What type of prompt was Jonah given?
   - ① Personal narrative
   - ② Informational expository
   - ③ Persuasive
   - ④ Fictional narrative

2. What are some cue words in the prompt that indicate Jonah's purpose for writing?
   - ① Everyone has had
   - ② …when you felt
   - ③ Think about
   - ④ Write to tell about

3. What type of plan did Jonah create?
   - ① Storyboard
   - ② Timeline
   - ③ Web
   - ④ Outline

4. Why is this type of plan appropriate for this prompt?
   - ① It arranges events in time order.
   - ② It groups related details into separate paragraphs.
   - ③ It identifies both similarities and differences.
   - ④ This is not an appropriate type of plan.

5. Which of the following details would **NOT** fit into Jonah's plan?
   - ① Kids were teasing me about the wrong bus at lunchtime.
   - ② My little sister's birthday party will be next Saturday.
   - ③ My face turned red when I realized I was on the wrong bus.
   - ④ From now on, I plan to check the bus number before getting on the bus.

6. Which of the following would make a good title for Jonah's piece?
   - ① My First Day of Kindergarten
   - ② The Lazy Days of Summer
   - ③ My Embarrassing Trip to Middle School
   - ④ Listen to Your Mom's Advice

7. What is the **main idea** of Jonah's story?

   ① Jonah was embarrassed the day he got on the wrong bus.

   ② Jonah is tired in the mornings.

   ③ Jonah and his friends eat lunch together.

   ④ It's fun to try out different buses and meet new friends.

8. Which of the following would **NOT** be a good way for Jonah to begin his story?

   ① Have you ever had a really embarrassing experience? Let me tell you about my most embarrassing day ever.

   ② Everyone knows what it's like to feel embarrassed. I have had my share of embarrassing experiences – especially the day I got on the wrong bus!

   ③ Hello. My name is Jonah and I will tell you a story about me.

   ④ It seemed like a typical morning. Little did I know, it was the beginning of the most embarrassing day of my life.

9. Which of the following would make a good **ending** for Jonah's story?

   ① Just remember: check the bus number *before* you get on the bus.

   ② That is the end of my story about me.

   ③ Kids at lunch were really teasing me and I felt embarrassed.

   ④ I am out of things to say, so this is the end of my story.

10. Based on his plan, what point of view will Jonah use in his piece?

   ① Third person   ③ First person

   ② Second person   ④ He will not use a point of view.

ASSESSMENT 1, FORM A

Answer Key:

1. ①	2. ④	3. ②	4. ①	5. ②
6. ③	7. ①	8. ③	9. ①	10. ③

Purpose:

This assessment is designed to evaluate a student's ability to recognize the essential elements of planning a focused personal narrative piece.

Tips for Re-teaching:

- Share personal narratives with students and work together to list main events in order of occurrence.

- Provide an assortment of prompts and discuss the purpose of each. Point out key words in the prompt that are "purpose cues" (e.g., *Tell about a time, Write about a time, Tell the story of what happened when, Tell about when, etc.)*

- Tell the students a brief personal narrative story, and then allow them to help you create a timeline plan for writing your story.

- Provide a personal narrative prompt and practice listing events in the order in which they occurred. Guide students through the process of verbalizing the story in chronological order.

- Practice using a storyboard as a personal narrative planner. Many students will benefit from visual cues to help them order the events in a story.

- Compare various types of graphic organizers (e.g., outlines, timelines, boxes, flow charts, webs, storyboards). Discuss the purpose of each and guide students to the understanding that personal narrative writing is best organized in a linear planner that places events in chronological order.

- After guiding students through the planning process, allow students to work independently to plan a personal narrative piece.

- Explicitly teach students to read and comprehend questions. Have them restate the question in their own words to check comprehension.

- After re-teaching and independent practice, re-test the students.

> *Everyone can think of a time when they felt disappointed. Think about a time when you felt disappointed. Write to tell about your disappointing experience.*

Sarah's teacher gave this prompt to her, and Sarah created the following plan:

Morning: Woke up – day of beach party with friends, sunny
            Packed – sunscreen, towel, music, beach ball, etc.
            Dressed – new bathing suit, big t-shirt, flip flops, etc.
            Breakfast – breakfast bar, juice
            Called friends – plans: Mom driving, lunch, etc.

Noon: Jumped in van with bag, sky a little cloudy
            Mom driving to pick up four friends
            Sky kept getting darker
            Thunder – no beach trip – all disappointed
            Groans, long faces, a few tears

Afternoon: Mom called other moms
            Went back to my house
            Moved furniture, put out beach towels, put on music. Had
            picnic, pretended to be at beach, rented movie

Night: Went to bed listening to rain
            Realized it all turned out okay in the end

1. What type of prompt was Sarah given?

   ① Persuasive   ③ Personal narrative

   ② Informational expository   ④ Fictional narrative

2. What are some cue words in the prompt that indicate Sarah's **purpose** for writing?

   ① *Write to tell about*   ③ *Think about*

   ② *...when they felt*   ④ *Everyone can think*

3. What type of plan did Sarah create?

   ① Timeline   ③ Outline

   ② Storyboard   ④ Web

4. Why is this type of plan appropriate for this prompt?

   ① This is not an appropriate type of plan for this prompt.

   ② It groups related details into separate paragraphs.

   ③ It identifies both similarities and differences.

   ④ It arranges events in time order.

5. Which of the following details would **NOT** fit into Sarah's plan?

   ① I packed an extra beach towel in case someone else forgot.

   ② We forgot to check the weather forecast.

   ③ School days are perfect for spending time with your friends.

   ④ A low rumble of thunder seemed to be rolling toward us.

6. Which of the following would make a good **title** for Sarah's piece?

   ① A Perfect Winter's Day

   ② My Mom is a Crazy Driver

   ③ The Worst Night of My Life

   ④ The Indoor Beach Party

7. What is the **main idea** of Sarah's story?

    ① Sarah didn't like it when her mother planned parties.

    ② The weather ruined Sarah's beach party, but they had fun anyway.

    ③ Sarah and her friends had a picnic for lunch.

    ④ The weather is unpredictable.

8. Which of the following would **NOT** be a good way for Sarah to begin her story?

    ① Have you ever wanted to plan a beach party? Let me give you some advice: check the weather forecast before you make your plans.

    ② My name is Sarah and I want to tell you about me and my friends.

    ③ "Sarah! Time to get up!" my Mom called. I jumped out of bed, ready to greet the day I'd been waiting for.

    ④ It was supposed to be the best day ever, but it turned out to be the biggest disappointment ever – almost!

9. Which of the following would make a good **ending** for Sarah's story?

    ① Now I am finished and you can tell me about your disappointing day.

    ② There is no more room, so this is the end.

    ③ I guess I learned that a little disappointment doesn't have to ruin your day.

    ④ The beach is a fun place to play, even if my mom drives us there.

10. Based on her plan, what point of view will Sarah use in her piece?

    ① First person   ③ Third person

    ② Second person   ④ She will not use a point of view.

ASSESSMENT 1, FORM B

Answer Key:

1. ③	2. ①	3. ①	4. ④	5. ③
6. ④	7. ②	8. ②	9. ③	10. ①

Characters:

Sam: neighborhood kid
Merlin: Sam's golden retriever
Sam's mom
Strange neighbor

Setting:

Suburban neighborhood with sidewalks, houses side by side, fenced yards behind each house. Present time.

Plot:

1. Sam tells mother he's going out to play.

2. Plays fetch with golden retriever. Stick lands in new neighbor's yard.

3. Merlin jumps fence and goes in yard – doesn't return.

4. Sam goes to neighbor's door, scared. Neighbor answers, Sam comes out.

5. Sam is chewing dog biscuit she gave him.

6. Magical things start to happen: Sam jumps like he's flying, does flips in air, begins to talk to Sam.

7. Sam runs in to get Mom. Merlin is normal while Mom is around.

8. Continues for one day. Never happened again.

Carmen created this plan for a story she plans to write. Answer the following questions about Carmen's plan:

1. What is the purpose of the piece Carmen plans to write?

   ① To inform

   ② To entertain

   ③ To persuade

   ④ To explain

2. What type of piece is Carmen planning to write?

   ① Opinion/persuasive
   ② Personal narrative
   ③ Informational expository
   ④ Fictional narrative

3. This type of plan is appropriate because:

   ① It arranges events in time order.
   ② It groups related details into separate paragraphs.
   ③ It identifies both similarities and differences.
   ④ This is not an appropriate type of plan.

4. What is the probably the main idea of Carmen's piece?

   ① Dogs can learn to do many tricks if you work with them daily.
   ② Always tell a parent before you go out to play.
   ③ Sam's neighbor has magical powers that she passed to the dog.
   ④ Cats are better pets than dogs.

5. Who are the main characters in Carmen's piece?

   ① Sam and Mom
   ② Sam and Merlin
   ③ Merlin and the new neighbor
   ④ Sam and the new neighbor

6. Which of the following would make a good beginning for Carmen's piece?

   ① My name is Carmen and I am going to tell you a story.
   ② Hello. Have you ever met my dog? Well, I have.
   ③ "Mom, I'm headed outside to play with Merlin!" I called.
   ④ Dogs are the best pets and I will tell you why.

7. Which of the following would **NOT** be a good ending for Carmen's piece?

   ① I'll never forget the day that Merlin was magical.
   ② Merlin's name took on a new meaning after that magical day!
   ③ Now you know all about my dog, Merlin.
   ④ Everyone has had "magical" day, but mine was one for the record books!

8.   Which of the following details would **NOT** fit in Carmen's piece?

① Merlin had golden-brown fur and big, round eyes.

② The house next door seemed dark and eerie.

③ Sam's favorite subject in school was math.

④ Merlin's favorite game was fetch.

9.   Which part of Carmen's piece should contain the most details?

① Beginning

② Middle

③ End

④ All parts should have an equal number of details.

10.   What is Carmen's next step?

① Make a plan

② Illustrate her story

③ Present her story to the class

④ Write her story

Assessment 2, Form A

Answer Key:

1. ②	2. ④	3. ①	4. ③	5. ②
6. ③	7. ③	8. ③	9. ②	10. ④

Purpose:

This assessment is designed to evaluate a student's ability to recognize the essential elements of planning a focused fictional narrative piece.

Tips for Re-teaching:

- Provide an assortment of prompts and discuss the purpose of each. Point out key words in the prompt that are "purpose cues" (e.g., *Write a story about, tell about, write about a time, imagine..., write to explain, given reasons why, etc.*).

- Tell a familiar story or folk tale. Have students create storyboards to sequence the events of the familiar story. Practice adding appropriate beginnings and endings.

- Provide settings, characters and problems. Practice developing an ending for the story, and then list events that lead to that ending on the board or on chart paper. The ending should drive the events in a narrative piece.

- Generate various character and setting descriptions. Draw attention to the importance of descriptive details and point out how word choices can create different feelings and visual images for the reader.

- Compare various types of graphic organizers (e.g., outlines, timelines, boxes, flow charts, webs, storyboards). Discuss the purpose of each and guide students to the understanding that fictional narrative is best organized on a linear planner that places events in chronological order.

- After guiding students through the planning process, allow students to work independently to plan a fictional narrative piece.

- Explicitly teach students to read and comprehend questions. Have them restate the question in their own words to check comprehension.

- After re-teaching and independent practice, re-test the students.

Characters:

Percy: farmer's son
Walter: hired worker
Percy's dad
Doc Simmons

Setting:

Family farm. Mostly flat plains, a few hills, corn fields, long country roads, houses far apart.

Plot:

1. Percy's dad goes to meeting at bank – Percy and Walter left to work

2. Percy distracted, doesn't listen – Walter does most of the work

3. Percy wants to drive tractor – Walter says no – Percy refuses to help

4. Tractor turns over on Walter – Percy runs to Walter who is pinned down – calls for help, but no one can hear

5. Percy listens to Walter's directions – uses fence post as leverage to lift tractor just enough to slide Walter out

6. Percy apologizes – Walter forgives

7. Dad's truck returns – Percy flags him down – they put Walter in the truck bed and take him to the hospital. Walter will recover.

8. Percy learned the importance of following directions.

Milton created this graphic organizer for a story he plans to write. Answer the following questions about Milton's plan:

1. What is the purpose of the piece Milton plans to write?

   ① To entertain   ③ To inform

   ② To persuade   ④ To compare

2. What type of piece is Milton planning to write?

   ① Comparison   ③ Informational expository

   ② Opinion/persuasive   ④ Fictional narrative

3. This type of plan is appropriate because:

   ① This is not an appropriate type of plan.

   ② It groups related details into separate paragraphs.

   ③ It identifies both similarities and differences.

   ④ It arranges events in time order.

4. What is probably the main idea of Milton's piece?

   ① Percy's dad had an important meeting at the bank.

   ② Percy learned the value of following directions.

   ③ Walter was probably bossy.

   ④ People who live on family farms are lucky.

5. Who are the main characters in Milton's piece?

   ① Dad and Walter   ③ Walter and Percy

   ② Percy and Dad   ④ There are no main characters

6. Which of the following would make a good beginning for Milton's piece?

   ① My name is Milton and I am going to tell you a story.

   ② Hello. How are you? I'm fine. Would you like to hear a story?

   ③ Once upon a time there was a farm.

   ④ *Grrrr.* The old truck groaned as Percy's Dad eased it onto the road.

7. Which of the following would **NOT** be a good ending for Milton's piece?

    ① Everyone went to bed feeling relieved and thankful – especially Percy.

    ② That is the end of my story. I hope you liked it.

    ③ Percy looked into Walter's eyes and knew that he was forgiven.

    ④ Percy learned an important lesson that day – a lesson he'd never forget.

8. Which of the following details would **NOT** fit in Milton's piece?

    ① Percy knew his father was worried about keeping the old farm running.

    ② Walter was strong and wore his old straw hat like a crown.

    ③ Percy felt anger filling his chest and pulsing through his veins.

    ④ On Saturday, Percy planned to go fishing.

9. Which part of Milton's piece should contain the most details?

    ① Beginning

    ② Middle

    ③ End

    ④ All parts should have an equal number of details.

10. What is Milton's next step?

    ① Write his rough draft

    ② Make a plan

    ③ Illustrate his story

    ④ Publish his story

Assessment 2, Form B

Answer Key:

1. ①	2. ④	3. ④	4. ②	5. ③
6. ④	7. ②	8. ④	9. ②	10. ①

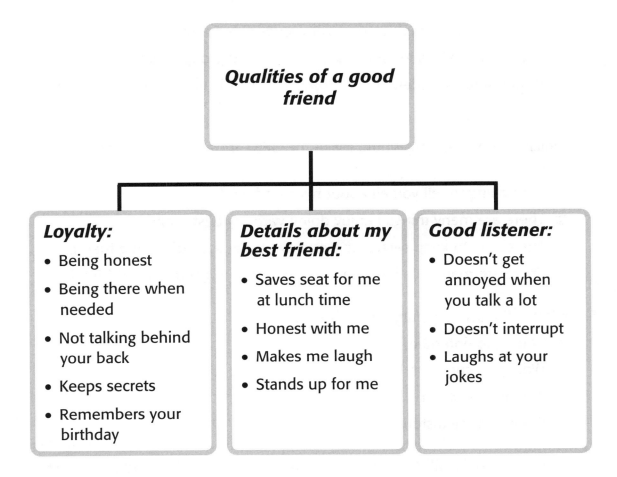

Gina created this plan after reading a prompt given to her by her teacher. Use Gina's plan to answer the following questions.

1. Which type of piece is Gina planning to write?
   ① Expository
   ② Personal narrative
   ③ Fictional narrative
   ④ Procedural

2. What is the topic of this piece?
   ① Loyalty
   ② Details about my best friend
   ③ Qualities of a good friend
   ④ Good listener

3. Why is this type of graphic organizer appropriate for this piece?

   ① It arranges details in time order.

   ② It puts steps in order.

   ③ It groups related details.

   ④ It is not appropriate for an expository piece.

4. Which of the following would make the **BEST** thesis statement for this piece?

   ① I am going to tell you all about my best friend.

   ② There are many things I enjoy doing with my best friend.

   ③ The ability to keep secrets is a quality I really appreciate in a friend.

   ④ There are many qualities that work together to make a good friend.

5. What is the primary purpose of this piece?

   ① Writing to entertain

   ② Writing to compare

   ③ Writing to explain

   ④ Writing to tell a story

6. Which sub-topic will make the strongest paragraph and should probably be used as the first body paragraph?

   ① Loyalty

   ② Details about my best friend

   ③ Qualities of a good friend

   ④ Good listener

7. Which sub-topic will make the weakest paragraph and, if used, should probably be the middle body paragraph?

   ① Loyalty

   ② Details about my best friend

   ③ Qualities of a good friend

   ④ Good listener

8. Which of the following details would probably not fit into this graphic organizer?

   ① Why I like pizza

   ② The time my best friend spent the night

   ③ Great sense of humor

   ④ Share a lot of the same interests

9. What would be an appropriate title for Gina's piece?

    ① The Gift of Friendship

    ② Gina's Guide to Surviving School

    ③ Why I Don't Like Sharon

    ④ Something You Should Know About Me

10. What is Gina's next step?

    ① Editing and revising

    ② Publishing her piece

    ③ Gathering data

    ④ Writing her rough draft

Answer Key:

1. ①	2. ③	3. ③	4. ④	5. ③
6. ①	7. ④	8. ①	9. ①	10. ④

Purpose:

This assessment is designed to evaluate a student's ability to recognize the essential elements of planning a focused expository piece.

Tips for Re-teaching:

- Provide an assortment of prompts and discuss the purpose of each. Point out key words in the prompt that are "purpose cues" (e.g., *Tell how, Explain why, Give reasons why, Tell about a time, Compare, Convince, Persuade, etc.*)

- Provide a prompt and practice listing details on sticky notes or small slips of paper. Guide students through the process of physical sorting – physically moving pieces of paper to group related details together.

- Once groups of related details have been sorted, create a rationale for each group and transfer the prompt, rationale, and details onto an appropriate graphic organizer.

- Assess the number and quality of details in each group and determine the best order for the body paragraphs. Generally, if writing three body paragraphs, it is advisable to put the strongest paragraph first and the weakest in the middle.

- Compare various types of graphic organizers (e.g., outlines, timelines, boxes, flow charts, webs, storyboards). Discuss the purpose of each and guide students to the understanding that most expository writing is best organized as groups of related details, not chronological order.

- After guiding students through the planning process, allow students to work independently to plan an informational expository piece.

- Explicitly teach students to read and comprehend questions. Have them restate the question in their own words to check comprehension.

- After re-teaching and independent practice, re-test the students.

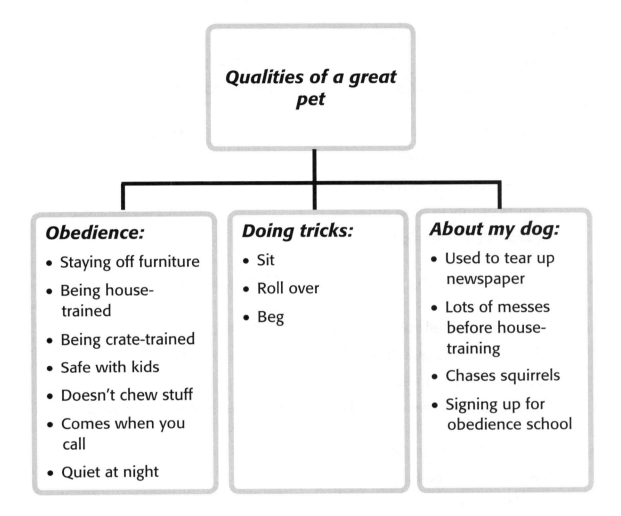

Qualities of a great pet

Obedience:
- Staying off furniture
- Being house-trained
- Being crate-trained
- Safe with kids
- Doesn't chew stuff
- Comes when you call
- Quiet at night

Doing tricks:
- Sit
- Roll over
- Beg

About my dog:
- Used to tear up newspaper
- Lots of messes before house-training
- Chases squirrels
- Signing up for obedience school

Jonathon created this plan after reading a prompt given to him by his teacher. Use Jonathon's graphic organizer to answer the following questions.

1. Which type of piece is Jonathon planning to write?

    ① Persuasive

    ② Personal narrative

    ③ Fictional narrative

    ④ Expository

2. What is the topic of this piece?

   ① Obedience   ③ Doing tricks

   ② Qualities of a great pet   ④ All about my dog

3. Why is this type of plan appropriate for an expository piece?

   ① It is not appropriate for an expository piece.

   ② It groups related details.

   ③ It puts events in time order.

   ④ It orders steps to a process.

4. Which of the following would make the **BEST** thesis statement for this piece?

   ① I am going to tell you all about my dog, Barney.

   ② There are many qualities to look for when selecting a pet.

   ③ Doing tricks is an important part of being a good pet.

   ④ There are many reasons make why dogs make better pets than cats.

5. What is the primary purpose of this piece?

   ① Writing to compare

   ② Writing to tell a story

   ③ Writing to explain

   ④ Writing to entertain

6. Which sub-topic will make the strongest paragraph and should probably be used as the first body paragraph?

   ① Obedience   ③ Qualities of a great pet

   ② Doing tricks   ④ About my dog

7. Which sub-topic will make the weakest paragraph and, if used, should probably be the middle body paragraph?

   ① Obedience   ③ Qualities of a great friend

   ② Doing tricks   ④ About my dog

8. Which of the following details would probably **NOT** fit into this graphic organizer?

    ① Pets need to be kind to visitors.

    ② My dog loves milk bones.

    ③ Beg, heel, bark, and fetch.

    ④ I can do magic tricks.

9. What would be an appropriate title for Jonathon's piece?

    ① The Cat from the Cosmos

    ② Why I Love Barney

    ③ Pointers for Finding the Perfect Pet

    ④ How to Train Your Dog

10. What is Jonathon's next step?

    ① Writing his rough draft

    ② Editing and revising

    ③ Publishing his piece

    ④ Gathering and organizing data

Answer Key:

1. ④	2. ②	3. ②	4. ②	5. ③
6. ①	7. ②	8. ④	9. ③	10. ①

José completed the following piece:

[1] My name is José and I will tell you about a time when I learned to do something new. [2] It was Christmas. [3] I was five years old. [4] I got a bike. [5] It had training wheels. [6] I like to ride my bike but my sister and brother made fun of me because of my training wheels. [7] I asked my uncle to take the training wheels off my bike. [8] He took them off and I tried to ride it. [9] I fell down many times. [10] My brother and sister laughed at me. [11] My brother plays football and soccer. [12] I fell one time and my knee was scraped. [13] They didn't laugh. [14] They started to help me. [15] My sister got a band-aid and my brother said he would hold the back of my bike to help me balance. [16] He was holding the bike and I was doing fine. [17] We did this many times down the driveway in front of our house. [18] My brother let go of the back of my bike and I did not know he let go. [19] I was riding by myself. [20] Now you know about a time I learned to do something new.

1. What type of piece has José written?
    ① Personal narrative
    ② Fictional narrative
    ③ Informational expository
    ④ Persuasive

2. What is the main idea of this piece?
    ① José does not like his brother and sister.
    ② José had a great Christmas when he was five years old.
    ③ José learned to ride his bike without training wheels.
    ④ This story does not have a main idea.

3. How can José improve sentence [1]?

   ① He needs to indent the first sentence.

   ② He needs to write a sentence that will grab the reader's attention.

   ③ He needs to introduce his brother and sister when he introduces himself.

   ④ He should not change sentence [1].

4. Which sentence is off-topic and should be removed from the piece?

   ① Sentence [6]

   ② Sentence [19]

   ③ Sentence [15]

   ④ Sentence [11]

5. Which of the following sentences could be added after sentence [17]?

   ① At first, he held on tight and I tried my best to keep the handlebars straight.

   ② I don't like playing soccer so I had nothing to do.

   ③ My uncle lives nearby and is always willing to help when I call him.

   ④ None of the above

6. Which of the following is missing in this piece?

   ① Transition words

   ② Main idea

   ③ Focus

   ④ Logical sequence of events

7. José wants to add this sentence to his piece:

   The bike was bright red with silver tassels hanging from the handlebars.

   After which sentence should José add this description?

   ① After sentence [1]

   ② After sentence [4]

   ③ After sentence [9]

   ④ After sentence [17]

8. José would like to add more details to his piece. Which type of details should he add?

   ① Details about his brother's sports adventures

   ② Details about the other Christmas presents he received

   ③ Details about how it feels to be the youngest child in the family

   ④ Details about how it felt to ride without training wheels

9. Which of the following should replace sentence [20] to make a stronger conclusion?

   ① That is the end of my story.

   ② Now you can tell me about a time you learned something new.

   ③ I'll never forget the day I learned to soar down the driveway on two wheels.

   ④ The conclusion is fine as it is.

10. What is José's next step?

   ① Revising his story to make sure it is clear and interesting

   ② Using a graphic organizer to make a plan

   ③ Editing spelling, capitalization and punctuation

   ④ Writing his rough draft

ASSESSMENT 4, FORM A

Answer Key:

1. ①	2. ③	3. ②	4. ④	5. ①
6. ①	7. ②	8. ④	9. ③	10. ①

Purpose:

This assessment is designed to evaluate a student's ability to recognize the elements of focus and organization in a personal narrative piece.

Tips for Re-teaching:

- Read personal narrative literature models and analyze features that demonstrate focus and organization.

- Re-teach, model, and practice writing various types of effective beginnings and endings.

- Work together to develop personal narrative prompts. Create verbal models of personal narratives in response to prompts. Allow students to respond verbally and tell personal narrative stories.

- Construct a personal narrative model that lacks elements of organization and focus. Allow students to lead you through the revision process to make your personal narrative model stronger.

- Create topics and present students with details. Students should identify which details are on-topic and which details are off-topic.

- Allow students to create personal timelines with drawings and/or photographs. Use the timelines as a plan for constructing a personal narrative.

- Create an experience for your students (e.g., a scavenger hunt, a kickball game, a service project, etc.). Demonstrate the development of a linear plan and write a brief personal narrative related to the shared experience. Allow students to develop their own personal narratives about the shared experience.

- Review test-taking skills.

- After re-teaching and independent practice, re-test the students.

Macy completed the following piece:

> [1] I will tell you about a special day. [2] One time my mom told me we were going to go for a ride. [3] She did not tell me where we were going. [4] After a short drive, we went to my aunt's house. [5] There were a lot of cars parked around her house. [6] We went to the door. [7] When it opened I saw that all of the family and many of my friends were there. [8] My best friend, Taylor, was standing right up front. [9] Taylor likes to play baseball. [10] Even though my birthday was still three days away, they were all there to give me a surprise party. [11] We played games, ate cake and then I opened presents.

1. What type of piece has Macy written?
   ① Persuasive
   ② Informational expository
   ③ Fictional narrative
   ④ Personal narrative

2. What is the **main idea** of this piece?
   ① Macy's surprise party made this day very special for her.
   ② Macy's mother does not like to stay home on Saturdays.
   ③ Taylor is a special friend.
   ④ This story does not have a main idea.

3. How can Macy improve sentence [1]?
   ① She needs to indent the first sentence.
   ② She needs to introduce Taylor in the first sentence.
   ③ She needs to write a sentence that will grab the reader's attention.
   ④ She should not change sentence [1].

4. Which sentence is off-topic and should be removed from the piece?

   ① Sentence [2]

   ② Sentence [7]

   ③ Sentence [9]

   ④ Sentence [11]

5. Which of the following sentences could be added after sentence [7]?

   ① That was the most special day ever.

   ② My eyes grew as big as saucers when they shouted, "Surprise!"

   ③ Sometimes we like to go for rides on Saturdays.

   ④ None of the above

6. Which of the following is missing in this piece?

   ① Transition words

   ② Main idea

   ③ Focus

   ④ Conclusion

7. Macy wants to add this sentence to her piece:

   I hopped in the car and buckled my seat belt, ready for an unknown adventure.

   After which sentence should Macy add this sentence?

   ① After sentence [1]

   ② After sentence [3]

   ③ After sentence [7]

   ④ After sentence [10]

8. Macy would like to add more details to her piece. Which type of details should she add?

   ① Details about the car

   ② Details about Taylor's baseball team

   ③ Details about the party

   ④ Details about what Macy wants for her birthday

9. Which of the following should be added after [11] to make a strong conclusion?

   ① That is all I have to tell you about my special day.

   ② It was the best birthday party ever!

   ③ The cake was chocolate inside, with white and green icing on top.

   ④ Now you can tell me about your special day.

10. What is Macy's next step?

   ① Using a graphic organizer to make a plan

   ② Editing spelling, capitalization and punctuation

   ③ Revising her story to make sure it is clear and interesting

   ④ Writing her rough draft

Assessment 4, Form B

Answer Key:

1. ④	2. ①	3. ③	4. ③	5. ②
6. ④	7. ②	8. ③	9. ②	10. ③

Carson wrote the following piece. Read Carson's piece and answer the questions that follow.

[1] I will tell you about my family. [2] We do many things together and enjoy being with each other.

[4] We like to go to the park on Saturdays and Sundays. [5] There is a park near our house. [6] It has swings, slides, and lots of structures for climbing. [7] We usually take our bats and gloves to the park and play a game of softball. [8] After that, we like to go out to lunch. [9] Our favorite place to eat is The Pizza Palace. [10] Then, my dad and mom like to watch sports on their big televisions. [11] My brother and I play checkers while we wait for our pizza. [12] My brother sometimes cheats at checkers, but he is younger than I am so I try to be patient. [13] When the pizza arrives, we all gobble it down. [14] We always talk and laugh together while we eat. [15] Weekends with my family are always lots of fun.

[16] Now you know why my family is very special to me.

1. What is the purpose of Carson's piece?
   ① She is writing to tell the reader about a personal experience.
   ② She is writing to persuade the reader that her family is better than others.
   ③ She is writing to tell why her family is special.
   ④ She is writing to compare herself to her brother.

2. Carson wants to change sentence [1] to improve the beginning of her piece. Which of the following sentences would make a more effective beginning?
   ① My mom, my dad, and my brother are very special to me.
   ② Do you like pizza?
   ③ My name is Carson and I am going to tell you about my family.
   ④ I can get mad at my brother sometimes.

3. Which of the following is an example of a transition Carson used in her piece?

    ① One time,

    ② First,

    ③ Last but not least,

    ④ After that,

4. Which sentence is off-topic and should be deleted?

    ① Sentence [2]

    ② Sentence [7]

    ③ Sentence [9]

    ④ Sentence [12]

5. Carson wants to add the following detail to her piece. Where should she place it?

    We used to bring the tee with us, but now my brother and I are good enough to hit our parents' pitches.

    ① After sentence [1]

    ② After sentence [7]

    ③ After sentence [12]

    ④ After sentence [16]

6. Carson wants to replace the word "Then" in sentence [10] with a different transition.

    Which of the following would be the best to replace "Then" in sentence [10]?

    ① On the other hand,

    ② After all,

    ③ While we wait for our pizza,

    ④ All of a sudden,

7. Which part of Carson's story should contain the greatest number of details?

    ① The beginning

    ② The middle

    ③ The end

    ④ None of the above

8. Which of the following would make a more effective ending for Carson's piece?

    ① That is the end of my story about my special family.

    ② My brother is such a pest.

    ③ There's no doubt about it; the people in my family are very special to me.

    ④ None of the above

9. Which of the following is a **detail** from Carson's piece?

    ① Carson's family enjoys being together.

    ② Carson's family is very special to her because they do things together.

    ③ The park has swings, slides, and structures for climbing.

    ④ None of the above

10. What is the **main idea** of Carson's piece?

    ① Carson's family enjoys pizza.

    ② Carson and her family enjoy going to the park.

    ③ Softball is Carson's favorite sport.

    ④ The people in Carson's family are special to her.

ASSESSMENT 5, FORM A

Answer Key:

1. ③	2. ①	3. ④	4. ④	5. ②
6. ③	7. ②	8. ③	9. ③	10. ④

Purpose:

This assessment is designed to evaluate a student's ability to recognize correctly applied organizational skills in a written composition. Organizational skills assessed include author's purpose, beginning and ending techniques, transitions, supporting details and focus.

Tips for Re-teaching:

- Read samples of the student's writing and identify common error patterns in organization. If the student's error patterns are aligned with errors on this assessment, focus instruction on these specific skills. If the student's error patterns are not aligned with errors on this assessment, focus on test-taking strategies.

- Ask the student to revise this piece by adding a beginning technique, transitions, and additional details.

- Provide the student with resource lists of various types of beginning techniques and transitions.

- Have the student construct a plan, such as a list of events, timeline, or storyboard for this piece.

- Read this piece out loud to the student and allow the student to revise verbally while listening.

- Work with the student to create alternate beginnings and endings for this piece.

- Ask the student to identify the main idea of this piece.

- Instruct the student to highlight the details included in this piece. Discuss the way each detail supports or does not support the main idea.

- Explicitly teach students to read and comprehend questions. Have them restate the question in their own words to check comprehension.

- After re-teaching and independent practice, re-test the students.

Isaiah wrote the following report about the planet Mercury. Read Isaiah's report and answer the questions that follow.

[1] Do you know about Mercury? [2] Well, I know about Mercury and I will tell you all about what I know.

[3] First of all, Mercury is the closest planet to the sun. [4] It is the fastest planet. [5] I like to be fast and I am the fastest person in my class. [6] Mercury orbits the sun in only 88 days. [7] This is much faster than Earth, which orbits the sun in about 365 days. [8] Mercury is a very small planet and it has very little atmosphere. [9] This might be one reason why Mercury is covered with craters. [10] Mercury does not have a moon like the other planets in our Solar System. [11] From Earth, Mercury looks like a star in the sky. [12] It can be seen during the early morning or at twilight. [13] Scientists study Mercury through high-powered telescopes. [14] Using these telescopes, scientists have been able to create maps of Mercury's surface. [15] We have learned even more about Mercury by sending the Mariner 10 and Messenger spacecrafts near this unique planet.

[16] Now you know all about Mercury. [17] Would you like to tell me about a planet you have studied?

1. What is the purpose of Isaiah's piece?
   ① He is writing to tell the reader about a personal experience.
   ② He is writing to persuade the reader to study Mercury.
   ③ He is writing to inform the reader about Mercury.
   ④ He is writing to compare Mercury to Earth.

2. Which of the following sentences should replace sentences [1] and [2] to improve the beginning of his piece?

   ① What's fast, small, and covered with craters? The answer is Mercury, a unique and fascinating planet.

   ② Do you like to study planets? Well, I do.

   ③ My name is Isaiah and I am going to tell you all about Mercury.

   ④ None of the above

3. Which of the following is an example of a transition Isaiah used in his piece?

   ① To begin with,

   ② First of all,

   ③ All of a sudden,

   ④ Isaiah did not use any transitions.

4. Which sentence is off-topic and should be deleted?

   ① Sentence [3]

   ② Sentence [5]

   ③ Sentence [9]

   ④ Sentence [11]

5. Isaiah's teacher wants him to add some descriptive details to his piece. Which of the following would be a good place to add descriptive details?

   ① After sentence [1]

   ② After sentence [5]

   ③ After sentence [9]

   ④ None of the above

6. What type of detail did Isaiah use in sentences [6] and [7]?

   ① He quoted an expert.

   ② He used a definition.

   ③ He told a mini-story.

   ④ He made a comparison.

7. Which part of Isaiah's report should contain the greatest number of details?

    ① All parts should have the same number of details.

    ② The end of the report should contain the greatest number of details.

    ③ The middle of the report should contain the greatest number of details.

    ④ The beginning of the report should contain the greatest number of details.

8. Which of the following would make a more effective ending for Isaiah's report?

    ① Now you know why Mercury is my favorite planet in the Solar System. What is your favorite planet?

    ② That is the end of my report about the planet Mercury.

    ③ Even though it's small, Mercury is one of the most unique and fascinating planets in our Solar System.

    ④ None of the above

9. Which of the following sentences contains a **detail** about Mercury?

    ① Sentence [1]

    ② Sentence [2]

    ③ Sentence [6]

    ④ Sentence [16]

10. What is the **main idea** of Isaiah's piece?

    ① Mercury is a unique and interesting planet.

    ② Mercury would be a better place to live than Earth.

    ③ Mercury is Isaiah's favorite planet.

    ④ Earth is still the best planet for living things.

ASSESSMENT 5, FORM B

Answer Key:

1. ③	2. ①	3. ②	4. ②	5. ③
6. ④	7. ③	8. ③	9. ③	10. ①

Chapter Two
Style and Composition

Style and composition skills are the aesthetic qualities that bring pleasure and enjoyment to the reader. These are the skills used by writers to connect with the audience and build visual descriptions. Style and composition skills can be categorized into three main groups:

- word choice
- descriptive language
- sentence fluency

Word Choice

Word choice refers to the specific types of words used by an author to create an effect. They may elicit a visual image, create a mood, or add voice to a piece of writing. Word choice skills include: strong verbs, alliteration, onomatopoeia, transitions, dialogue tags, and pronouns that address the reader.

Descriptive Language

Descriptive language creates visual images for the reader and provides specific details that deepen a reader's understanding of the writer's purpose and message. A piece that lacks descriptive language is usually not engaging and leaves the reader with only general impressions instead of a clear vision of the author's purpose and intent. Descriptive language skills include: descriptive attributes, specificity, hyperbole, personification, simile, and metaphor.

Sentence Fluency

Sentence fluency can span both composition and convention skills. However, for our purposes in this chapter, we will refer to the rhythm and variation in sentences that can keep a reader engaged. Sentence fluency skills that add to the style and composition of a piece include: sentence variation, dialogue and embedded definitions.

Evaluating Style and Composition Skills

Written pieces that lack style and composition skills are flat and uninteresting to the reader. These pieces offer information devoid of visual description and relevant details. They may be well organized and employ perfect spelling, usage and handwriting; however, these pieces are not engaging and do not evoke a personal response from the reader.

Through multiple-choice tests, teachers can assess a student's knowledge of literary terms and techniques. Being able to identify these skills and being able to generate them in original pieces are, of course, two distinct processes. However, if students cannot identify these skills in writing, it is highly unlikely they will be able to use them in original compositions.

Assessments

In this section, the assessments are not genre-specific. These skills span all genres and should be used to create lively, engaging text. While purpose and audience should guide a writer's style, word choice, descriptive language, and sentence fluency can be infused into all writing.

The assessments in this chapter follow the pattern of the previous assessments. There are self-contained multiple-choice questions in the first series of tests and multiple-choice items addressing a written sample in the second series of tests. Each assessment contains ten items for ease of scoring.

Re-teaching and Re-testing

As in the previous chapter, each assessment contains a Form A and Form B. Form A is designed to be a diagnostic tool. After each Form A assessment, you will find an answer key, followed by re-teaching tips and strategies to address the skills presented in the test questions. For further information and reading that can yield additional strategies, a brief bibliography of professional books and a cross-index of literature models are supplied in the Resources.

Form B presents the student with the same types of questions and covers the same skills. This test is designed to assess student mastery after re-teaching intervention has occurred. If a student does not miss any items on the Form A assessment, it is not necessary to proceed with the re-teaching and re-testing.

Assessments – Style and Composition Skills

Assessment 6: Identifying word choice skills
> Form A
> Form B

Assessment 7: Identifying descriptive language skills
> Form A
> Form B

Assessment 8: Identifying sentence fluency skills
> Form A
> Form B

Assessment 9: Analyzing word choice skills in a written piece
> Form A
> Form B

Assessment 10: Analyzing descriptive language in a written piece
> Form A
> Form B

Assessment 11: Analyzing sentence fluency in a written piece
> Form A
> Form B

1. Which of these words is **NOT** a word that can be substituted for "said" in a dialogue tag?

    ① shouted   ③ whispered

    ② gold   ④ asked

2. **The wintry wind worked its way through the woods.**
   This sentence contains an example of:

    ① Dialogue   ③ Alliteration

    ② Strong verbs   ④ Onomatopoeia

3. **The car eeked and erked its way to a stop.**
   This sentence contains an example of:

    ① Dialogue   ③ Alliteration

    ② Strong verbs   ④ Onomatopoeia

4. **"Do not to wake the sleeping dragon," the princess _____ as she tip-toed past the snoring monster.**
   Which of the following would be the **best** way to complete the dialogue tag?

    ① shouted   ③ whispered

    ② said   ④ asked

5. Which of the following sentences uses **pronouns** to connect to the reader?

    ① One should always read the directions before using new equipment.

    ② A person using new equipment should be sure to read the directions first.

    ③ You should always read the directions before you use any new equipment.

    ④ Anyone using new equipment should read the directions first.

6. Which of the following sentences contains **strong verbs**?

    ① The boy sputtered and gasped for air as he crawled out of the water.

    ② The boy came out of the water and went onto the land safely.

    ③ The boy was in the water, and then he came out of the water.

    ④ The boy was trying to get his breath when he came out of the water.

7. Which of the following sentences does **NOT** contain **strong verbs**?

    ① The horse galloped across the pasture and then trotted into the stable.

    ② The large, beautiful, brown horse was in the tall, dark stable.

    ③ The sun glistened on the back of the horse as he paraded across the field.

    ④ The horse whinnied and neighed when he spotted the playful children.

8. Which group of words would most likely be used as **transition words**?

    ① The, and, but, or

    ② Talked, sang, laughed, giggled

    ③ Shining gems, sparkling water

    ④ To begin with, after that, finally

9. Which of the following transitions does **NOT** signal a time change?

    ① After dinner...   ③ My first reason...

    ② By noon...   ④ Later that day...

10. Which of the following transitions does **NOT** tell how to order steps in a procedure?

    ① The second step...

    ② Suddenly...

    ③ After you have gathered your materials...

    ④ The last thing you will do...

ASSESSMENT 6, FORM A

Answer Key:

1. ②	2. ③	3. ④	4. ③	5. ③
6. ①	7. ②	8. ④	9. ③	10. ②

Purpose:

This assessment is designed to evaluate a student's ability to recognize specific types of word choice made by an author to create interest and style in a written piece.

Tips for Re-teaching:

- Share literature models that provide examples of well-crafted word choice, including strong verbs, alliteration, onomatopoeia, pronouns, transition words and dialogue tags.

- Provide an assortment of prompts and discuss the purpose of each. Provide examples of ways to use well-crafted word choice in different types of writing.

- Isolate skills that are targeted for improvement. Teach these skills explicitly, show samples from literature models, and assign short, concise practice pieces for specific skills.

- Teach skills explicitly and then have students search through literature models to find examples of the specific skills taught.

- Examine drafts of previously written pieces and help students find opportunities to revise these pieces by adding word choice skills.

- If students continue to have difficulty with specific word choice skills, offer additional support by conducting guided and tandem writing activities.

- Provide examples and non-examples of word choice skills to help students refine their understanding of specific skills.

- Explicitly teach students to read and comprehend questions. Have them restate the question in their own words to check comprehension. Advise students to read all answer choices before selecting a response.

- After re-teaching and independent practice, re-test the students.

1. Which of these words can be substituted for "said" in a dialogue tag?

   ① Kept   ③ Answered

   ② Heard   ④ Talking

2. **A mosquito buzzed in my ear.**

   This sentence contains an example of:

   ① Dialogue   ③ Alliteration

   ② Strong verbs   ④ Onomatopoeia

3. **The lazy llama lived in on Lovely Lane.**

   This sentence contains an example of:

   ① Dialogue   ③ Alliteration

   ② Hyperbole   ④ Onomatopoeia

4. **"Yippee!!!" _____ the excited boy.**

   Which of the following would be the **best** way to complete the dialogue tag?

   ① shouted   ③ asked

   ② whispered   ④ said

5. Which of the following sentences uses **pronouns** to connect to the reader?

   ① You should feed your pet at the same time each day.

   ② One should feed a pet at the same time each day.

   ③ A pet owner should feed his or her pet at the same time each day.

   ④ A pet should be fed by the pet's owner at the same time each day.

6. Which sentence does **NOT** contain a **strong verb**?

   ① I raced to school.   ③ I pedaled to school.

   ② I went to school.   ④ I marched to school.

7. Which of the following sentences contains **strong verbs**?

   ① The tiny kitten was as scared as a mouse.

   ② The small, fearful kitten went under the big, red sofa.

   ③ The kitten trembled as it peered out from under the sofa.

   ④ Kittens can be so jumpy sometimes!

8. Which group of words are **NOT** transition words?

   ① For starters, on another note, last but not least

   ② Before sunrise, after breakfast, at noon time

   ③ Rocky cliffs, the green valley, pouring rain

   ④ On the other hand, another point to consider, also

9. Which of the following transitions signals a time change?

   ① At sunset...

   ② The next step...

   ③ The first reason...

   ④ You should also consider...

10. Which transition word would **probably not** be used in an expository piece?

   ① Furthermore...

   ② Suddenly...

   ③ First...

   ④ Finally...

Assessment 6, Form B

Answer Key:

1. ③	2. ④	3. ③	4. ①	5. ①
6. ②	7. ③	8. ③	9. ①	10. ②

1. Erica wants to use adjectives to describe clouds. Which list of adjectives would be best for describing clouds?

   ① rough, scratchy, solid

   ② loud, grainy, high-pitched

   ③ fluffy, white, translucent

   ④ dry, sharp, bitter

2. Julian would like to add a specific detail to this sentence:

   I ate <u>breakfast</u> and left for school.

   Which of the following could be substituted for the word "breakfast" in order to add a specific detail to the sentence?

   ① Lunch   ③ A breakfast meal

   ② Maple-flavored oatmeal   ④ Some food

3. **The stars twinkled like dancing fireflies in the night sky.**

   This sentence contains an example of a(an):

   ① Metaphor   ③ Hyperbole

   ② Simile   ④ Specificity

4. **Mrs. Smith was a brick wall, unyielding to our requests.**

   This sentence contains an example of a(an):

   ① Metaphor   ③ Hyperbole

   ② Simile   ④ Specificity

5. Which of the following sentences contains an example of **hyperbole**?

   ① My backpack weighed about a million pounds.

   ② Sarah's dog was only about a foot long.

   ③ My dad reached up on the top shelf and put the plates away.

   ④ I pedaled my bike quickly and tried to get to school on time.

6. Which sentence contains **specific** details?

    ① I plan to go to a picnic with friends from a club.

    ② The Saddle Club picnic will be held at White Oak Park.

    ③ The picnic will be held in the park.

    ④ My club is having a fun picnic at a park.

7. Which of the following phrases contains a **simile**?

    ① ...as soft as a rose petal.

    ② ...we like to play outside.

    ③ ...as I walked toward the setting sun.

    ④ ...soft and velvety smooth.

8. Which of the following phrases contains a **metaphor**?

    ① You are as strong as an ox!

    ② She's a ticking time bomb.

    ③ The sky was a soothing shade of blue.

    ④ She ran around like a dog chasing its tail.

9. Kara wants to add an adverb to this sentence to tell how the kittens were crying:

    The frightened kittens were crying _____.

    Which of the following adverbs would be the best choice to add to this sentence to tell **how** the kittens were crying?

    ① well   ③ carefully

    ② pitifully   ④ quickly

10. **The alarm clock screamed with a shrill voice.**

    This sentence contains an example of:

    ① Simile   ③ Adverbs

    ② Hyperbole   ④ Personification

Answer Key:

1. ③	2. ②	3. ②	4. ①	5. ①
6. ②	7. ①	8. ②	9. ②	10. ④

Purpose:

This assessment is designed to evaluate a student's ability to recognize descriptive language and descriptive devices used by an author to help the reader visualize text.

Tips for Re-teaching:

- Share literature models that provide examples of well-crafted descriptive language, including simile, metaphor, specificity, personification and descriptive attributes.

- Display an object or picture prompt and ask students to write a five-sentence description. Evaluate descriptive language used by the students. Make suggestions for specific types of descriptive devices students can add to their pieces.

- Provide an assortment of prompts and discuss the purpose of each. Provide examples of ways to use descriptive language in different types of writing.

- Isolate skills that are targeted for improvement. Teach these skills explicitly, show samples from literature models, and assign short, concise practice pieces for specific descriptive writing skills.

- Teach skills explicitly and then have students search through literature models to find examples of the specific skills taught.

- Examine drafts of previously written pieces and help students find opportunities to revise these pieces by adding descriptive language.

- Explicitly teach students to read and comprehend questions. Have them restate the question in their own words to check comprehension. Advise students to read all answer choices before selecting a response.

- After re-teaching and independent practice, re-test the students.

1. Kim wants to use adjectives to describe her favorite food. Which adjectives would be best for describing her favorite food?

    ① Scrumptious and delicious

    ② Sour and acrid

    ③ Graceful and athletic

    ④ Careful and cautious

2. Which sentence contains specific details about a family vacation?

    ① We went to a theme park, the beach and a shopping mall.

    ② We stayed at a hotel and then visited many interesting places.

    ③ We went to fabulous theme parks and wonderful stores on our family vacation.

    ④ We went to St. Augustine Beach, Ocean World and Paradise Mall.

3. **Books are my windows to worlds I have never seen.**

    This sentence contains an example of:
    ① Metaphor   ③ Specificity
    ② Simile   ④ Hyperbole

4. **The car rattled like tin cans bouncing down a sliding board.**

    This sentence contains an example of:
    ① Metaphor   ③ Specificity
    ② Simile   ④ Hyperbole

5. Which of the following sentences contains an example of **hyperbole**?

    ① The trees shaded us from the bright sun.

    ② The dog snarled and snapped at the playful squirrel.

    ③ I'm so tired I could sleep for about three months straight.

    ④ I rushed into the house when I heard my mother calling.

6. Which sentence contains **specific** details?

    ① I ate a roasted turkey sandwich with spicy mustard and cheddar cheese.

    ② My sandwich was really, really good and I liked it a lot.

    ③ I ate my lunch and enjoyed it.

    ④ During lunch, I enjoyed eating my favorite kind of sandwich.

7. Which of the following phrases contains a **simile**?

    ① Like I said before…

    ② As soon as I get home…

    ③ Like a scared rabbit in a sudden storm…

    ④ As the tall man entered the restaurant…

8. Which of the following phrases contains a **metaphor**?

    ① "Your room is a pig pen!" shouted Mom.

    ② "Your room is such a mess," said Mom.

    ③ "Clean up this mess!" commanded Mom.

    ④ "Your room looks like a tornado hit it," said Mom.

9. James wants to use an adverb to tell **how** he and his siblings played together.

    We were always able to play _____.

    Which of the following adverbs would be the best choice to add to this sentence to tell **how** the children played?

    ① Smoothly   ③ Always

    ② Cooperatively   ④ Sadly

10. **The raindrops dove angrily into puddles on the sidewalk.**

    This sentence contains an example of:

    ① Metaphor   ③ Simile

    ② Personfication   ④ Hyperbole

Assessment 7, Form B

Answer Key:

1. ①   2. ④   3. ①   4. ②   5. ③
6. ①   7. ③   8. ①   9. ②   10. ②

1. Erin wrote the following sentence:

   The dog trotted across the lawn.

   This is an example of a(n):
   ① Interrogative sentence
   ② Declarative sentence
   ③ Imperative sentence
   ④ Exclamatory sentence

2. Javier wrote this sentence:

   What secrets lurked in the dust-covered boxes of my grandmother's attic?

   This is an example of a(n):
   ① Interrogative sentence
   ② Declarative sentence
   ③ Imperative sentence
   ④ Exclamatory sentence

3. Kathleen wrote this sentence:

   What a beautiful day!

   This is an example of a(n):
   ① Interrogative sentence
   ② Declarative sentence
   ③ Imperative sentence
   ④ Exclamatory sentence

4. Sarah wrote this sentence:

   Read all of the directions before you begin building your project.

   This is an example of a(n):
   ① Interrogative sentence
   ② Declarative sentence
   ③ Imperative sentence
   ④ Exclamatory sentence

5. Which sentence is an example of **dialogue**?
   ① We read Joyce Kilmer's "Trees" during our program.
   ② "Always put forth your best effort," the teacher advised.
   ③ Our camp leader led us in singing "Row, Row, Row Your Boat."
   ④ I woke up early on Saturday morning and fixed my own breakfast.

6. Which sentence contains a definition?
   ① Jane, I wonder if you should pack an umbrella.
   ② "Keep a positive attitude," my mother stated cheerfully.
   ③ The twins often quarreled, or argued, with each other.
   ④ We make several pumpkin pies each Thanksgiving.

7. Which sentence contains a definition?
   ① She was praised for her congeniality (friendliness) by the other contestants.
   ② The cat crouched low, waiting to pounce on the unsuspecting puppy.
   ③ Gather all of your materials before you begin working.
   ④ The clouds were dark and low as the storm moved closer.

8. Keisha wrote these sentences:

   I like oranges. I like apples. I like bananas.

   Keisha could probably improve her piece by:
   ① Combining these three sentences
   ② Adding more sentences about other fruits she likes
   ③ Taking out the sentence about bananas
   ④ None of the above

9. Which of the following is a compound sentence?
   ① The large, blue truck sped out of the parking lot.
   ② Our neighbor has a dog and a cat.
   ③ My brother likes to watch football, but I like to watch baseball.
   ④ While the paint is drying, begin soaking the paintbrushes in water.

10. Which of the following is a complex sentence?
    ① The large, blue truck sped out of the parking lot.
    ② Our neighbor has a dog and a cat.
    ③ My brother likes to watch football, but I like to watch baseball.
    ④ While the paint is drying, begin soaking the paintbrushes in water.

Answer Key:

1. ②	2. ①	3. ④	4. ③	5. ②
6. ③	7. ①	8. ①	9. ③	10. ④

Purpose:

This assessment is designed to evaluate a student's ability to recognize and apply sentence fluency skills.

Tips for Re-teaching:

- Share literature models that provide examples of various sentence types, lengths and structures.

- Offer simple sentences to students and ask them to extend sentences by adding phrases that address where, when, why and/or how.

- Model and practice combining short, related sentences and segmenting run-on sentences.

- Provide an example of a paragraph with repetitive sentence length and structure. Work with students to revise the paragraph for sentence fluency and variation.

- Provide an assortment of prompts and discuss the purpose of each. Provide examples of ways to use different types of sentences.

- Teach sentence fluency skills explicitly, show samples from literature models, and assign short, concise practice pieces for sentence fluency skills.

- Teach skills explicitly and then have students search through literature models to find examples of the specific skills taught.

- Examine drafts of previously written pieces and help students find opportunities to revise these pieces by varying sentence structures.

- Explicitly teach students to read and comprehend questions. Have them restate the question in their own words to check comprehension. Advise students to read all answer choices before selecting a response.

- After re-teaching and independent practice, re-test the students.

1. Anderson wrote the following sentence:

   Who will be able to solve the mystery?

   This is an example of a(n):
   ① Interrogative sentence
   ② Declarative sentence
   ③ Imperative sentence
   ④ Exclamatory sentence

2. Tucker wrote this sentence:

   Man, did I ever feel silly!

   This is an example of a(n):
   ① Interrogative sentence
   ② Declarative sentence
   ③ Imperative sentence
   ④ Exclamatory sentence

3. Kathleen wrote this sentence:

   The man is waiting patiently.

   This is an example of a(n):
   ① Interrogative sentence
   ② Declarative sentence
   ③ Imperative sentence
   ④ Exclamatory sentence

4. Sarah wrote this sentence:

   Move quickly to a safe place when the storm begins.

   This is an example of a(n):
   ① Interrogative sentence
   ② Declarative sentence
   ③ Imperative sentence
   ④ Exclamatory sentence

5. Which sentence is an example of **dialogue**?
   ① Her favorite Christmas carol is "Jingle Bells."
   ② He wondered why the birds were silent.
   ③ We memorized a poem called "Snow."
   ④ "Would you like to go for a swim?" asked Dad.

6. Which sentence contains a definition?
   ① A barometer, a device used to measure air pressure, sat by the window.
   ② Fall is my favorite time of the year.
   ③ The trouble started when my brother walked through the door.
   ④ Do you have a dictionary?

7. Which sentence contains a definition?
   ① Keep a stiff upper lip and keep moving forward.
   ② Pine cones were scattered randomly across the forest floor.
   ③ A sudden surge – or strong, forward movement – frightened us.
   ④ The earth's orbit around the sun occurs over the course of one year.

8. Marcella wrote these sentences:

   I have a sister. She is kind. She is generous.

   Marcella could probably improve her piece by:
   ① Writing about her brother
   ② Changing "kind" to "nice"
   ③ Combining these sentences
   ④ None of the above

9. Which of the following is a compound sentence?
   ① My mother mowed the lawn and my dad trimmed the hedge.
   ② I like to play soccer and baseball.
   ③ As I walked through the door, I smelled brownies cooking in the oven.
   ④ Sam lives two blocks from my house.

10. Which of the following is a complex sentence?
    ① My mother mowed the lawn and my dad trimmed the hedge.
    ② I like to play soccer and baseball.
    ③ As I walked through the door, I smelled brownies cooking in the oven.
    ④ Sam lives two blocks from my house.

ASSESSMENT 8, FORM B

Answer Key:

1. ①	2. ④	3. ②	4. ③	5. ④
6. ①	7. ③	8. ③	9. ①	10. ③

Read this piece and answer the questions that follow:

"Taking Care of Your Teeth"

[1] *Click!* [2] A beautiful smile is a work of art. [3] Take care of your teeth, and you will be able to enjoy your own personal work of art for a lifetime.

[4] Most people know that they should brush after each meal, but there is more to taking care of your teeth than just brushing. [5] Proper home care includes fearless flossing and fierce flouride as well! [6] You should not be afraid to floss. [7] If you floss daily, your gums will be as tough as leather and you will remove bits of food caught between teeth. [8] As for brushing, be sure to scrub those teeth with flouride toothpaste, because flouride protects teeth from harmful bacteria that can cause decay.

[9] Another important part of good dental care is visiting your dentist twice a year. [10] The dentist uses special equipment that buzzes along your teeth to make them extra clean and shiny. [11] Dentists also make x-rays to be sure your teeth are healthy beneath the surface. [12] As my dentist likes to say, "Regular dental appointments will keep your teeth strong and healthy."

[13] Just remember, daily brushing and flossing will keep your teeth in tip-top shape, and regular visits to the dentist will ensure a healthy smile for years to come! [14] So don't be afraid to smile for the cameras. [15] *Click!*

1. Sentence [5] contains an example of:
   ① Onomatopoeia
   ② Alliteration
   ③ A dialogue tag
   ④ A transition

2. Sentence [8] contains an example of:
    ① A dialogue tag
    ② Onomatopoeia
    ③ Strong verbs
    ④ Pronouns

3. Sentence [9] contains an example of:
    ① A dialogue tag
    ② A transition
    ③ Onomatopoeia
    ④ Alliteration

4. Sentence [10] contains an example of:
    ① A dialogue tag
    ② A transition
    ③ Onomatopoeia
    ④ Alliteration

5. Sentence [12] contains an example of:
    ① A dialogue tag
    ② Alliteration
    ③ Onomatopoeia
    ④ None of the above

6. What types of words does the author use to address the reader in this piece?
    ① Dialogue tags
    ② Transitions
    ③ Strong verbs
    ④ Pronouns

7. Which of the following sentences does **NOT** contain a strong verb?

    ① Sentence [2]

    ② Sentence [7]

    ③ Sentence [8]

    ④ Sentence [13]

8. Which of the following sentences does **NOT** contain a transition?

    ① Sentence [8]

    ② Sentence [9]

    ③ Sentence [10]

    ④ Sentence [13]

9. What type of beginning technique does the author use in sentence [1]?

    ① Onomatopoeia

    ② Alliteration

    ③ Dialogue

    ④ A question

10. Which of the following sentences contains a pronoun?

    ① Sentence [5]

    ② Sentence [6]

    ③ Sentence [8]

    ④ Sentence [14]

Answer Key:

1. ②	2. ③	3. ②	4. ③	5. ①
6. ④	7. ①	8. ③	9. ①	10. ②

Purpose:

This assessment is designed to evaluate a student's ability to recognize word choice skills in a written piece. Word choice skills include strong verbs, alliteration, onomatopoeia, transitions, dialogue tags, and pronouns used to address the reader.

Tips for Re-teaching:

- Share literature models that provide examples of well-crafted word choice, including strong verbs, alliteration, onomatopoeia, pronouns, transition words and dialogue tags.

- Provide an assortment of prompts and discuss the purpose of each. Provide examples of ways to use well-crafted word choice in different types of writing.

- Isolate skills that are targeted for improvement. Teach these skills explicitly, show samples from literature models, and assign short, concise practice pieces for specific skills.

- Teach skills explicitly and then have students search through literature models to find examples of the specific skills taught.

- Examine drafts of previously written pieces and help students find opportunities to revise these pieces by adding word choice skills.

- If students continue to have difficulty with specific word choice skills, offer additional support by conducting guided and tandem writing activities.

- Provide examples and non-examples of word choice skills to help students refine their understanding of specific skills.

- Explicitly teach students to read and comprehend questions. Have them restate the question in their own words to check comprehension. Advise students to read all answer choices before selecting a response.

- After re-teaching and independent practice, re-test the students.

Read this piece and answer the questions that follow:

"My Sister"

[1] "Mom, tell her to get out of my room!" [2] This is something you can hear me shout on a daily basis. [3] My little sister won't leave me alone.

[4] First of all, there's her constant whining. [5] She tries to get her way by annoying everyone with her voice. [6] "Sarah, *please*!" she'll cry. [7] If I don't let her have her way, my mom will accuse me of being unreasonable. [8] Mom always says, "It's just a phase."

[10] My sister follows me around like my shadow on a sunny day. [11] She bursts into my room and stampedes through my personal stuff. [12] One time, she tripped over my shoes and knocked everything off of my dresser. [13] She is a catastrophe!

[14] Another annoying thing she does is pick up the phone to listen in on my conversations. [15] She thinks I can't hear the *blip* on the other end when she picks up the phone. [16] Then I'll hear her breathing and giggling while I talk to my friends. [17] She invades my privacy! [18] When my mom catches her, she has to hang up, but most of the time she doesn't get caught.

[19] If you have a little sister, you probably understand my problem. [20] If not, just call me. [21] I'll let you borrow my sister any time you like!

1. Sentence [1] is an example of:
    ① Onomatopoeia
    ② Alliteration
    ③ Tagless dialogue
    ④ A transition

2. Sentence [6] contains an example of:
    ① Onomatopoeia
    ② Alliteration
    ③ A dialogue tag
    ④ A transition

3. Sentence [11] contains an example of:
    ① A dialogue tag
    ② Onomatopoeia
    ③ Strong verbs
    ④ Alliteration

4. Sentence [15] contains an example of:
    ① A dialogue tag
    ② A transition
    ③ Onomatopoeia
    ④ Alliteration

5. Which of the following sentences does **NOT** contain a strong verb?
    ① Sentence [11]
    ② Sentence [13]
    ③ Sentence [16]
    ④ Sentence [17]

6. Which of the following sentences does **NOT** contain a transition?
    ① Sentence [4]
    ② Sentence [10]
    ③ Sentence [12]
    ④ Sentence [14]

7. In which sentence does the author use pronouns to address the reader?
   ① Sentence [3]
   ② Sentence [5]
   ③ Sentence [13]
   ④ Sentence [19]

8. Which of the following sentences does **NOT** contain a line of dialogue?
   ① Sentence [1]
   ② Sentence [6]
   ③ Sentence [8]
   ④ Sentence [17]

9. Which of the following words from this piece is **NOT** a strong verb?
   ① Accuse
   ② Stampedes
   ③ Conversations
   ④ Invades

10. What type of beginning technique does the author use in sentence [1]?
   ① Onomatopoeia
   ② Alliteration
   ③ Dialogue
   ④ A question

ASSESSMENT 9, FORM B

Answer Key:

1. ③   2. ③   3. ③   4. ③   5. ②

6. ②   7. ④   8. ④   9. ③   10. ③

PURPOSEFUL WRITING ASSESSMENT

Read this piece and answer the questions that follow:

"The Dog with Two Names"

[1] *Woof, woof!* [2] I heard a pitiful barking sound coming from behind a red maple tree. [3] I stepped off my bike, pulled the kick-stand down with one foot, and walked carefully around the tree. [4] That's when I spotted that poor dog. [5] He was sopping wet, trembling with fear, and gnawing on a hurt paw. [6] I didn't want to startle him, so I spoke softly and moved very slowly. [7] He responded to the sound of my voice, and so I invited him home with me. [8] "Come on, Sam, just follow my bike," I said gently. [9] He seemed to like that name and started limping along behind me like a reluctant shadow.

[10] When we got to my house, I let my bike fall into the grass and ran up the front porch steps in less than a second. [11] Sam cowered in the yard like an unwelcome party guest. [12] I returned with my mom, who was ready to make him feel right at home. [13] She is an angel of mercy for wounded animals. [14] Mom quickly found a large splinter wedged in Sam's paw and was able to remove it. [15] Sam licked her hand with gratitude. [16] As he did, a tag etched with the name *Barnie* peeked out from under his tangled fur. [17] On the back of the tag, a phone number jumped out at us. [18] Mom said, "This dog probably has a worried owner out there who will be happy to receive our call."

[19] In the end, we were able to return the lost dog to his grateful owners and everyone was happy. [20] Barnie and his owners found each other, while Mom and I found satisfaction in doing a good deed.

1. Sentence [2] contains which of the following?

   ① Simile

   ② Metaphor

   ③ Personification

   ④ Specific details

2. Which sentence uses adverbs to describe **how** something was done?

   ① Sentence [2]

   ② Sentence [4]

   ③ Sentence [6]

   ④ Sentence [9]

3. Sentence [9] contains which of the following?

   ① Simile

   ② Metaphor

   ③ Personification

   ④ Hyperbole

4. Sentence [10] contains which of the following?

   ① Simile

   ② Metaphor

   ③ Personification

   ④ Hyperbole

5. Sentence [11] contains which of the following?

   ① Simile

   ② Metaphor

   ③ Personification

   ④ Specific details

6. Sentence [13] contains which of the following?

   ① Simile

   ② Metaphor

   ③ Personification

   ④ Specific details

7. Sentence [16] contains which of the following?

   ① Simile

   ② Metaphor

   ③ Personification

   ④ Specific details

8. Sentence [17] contains which of the following?

   ① Simile

   ② Metaphor

   ③ Personification

   ④ Hyperbole

9. Which of the following sentences contains descriptive attributes?

   ① Sentence [1]

   ② Sentence [5]

   ③ Sentence [7]

   ④ Sentence [9]

10. Which words are used by the author to describe the dog's fur?

    ① trembling, gnawing

    ② limping, reluctant

    ③ wet, tangled

    ④ pitiful, grateful

ASSESSMENT 10, FORM A

Answer Key:

1. ④   2. ③   3. ①   4. ④   5. ①

6. ②   7. ③   8. ③   9. ②   10. ③

Purpose:

This assessment is designed to evaluate a student's ability to recognize descriptive language and descriptive devices used by an author to help the reader visualize text. Descriptive language skills include descriptive attributes (adjectives and adverbs), simile, metaphor, personification, hyperbole, and specificity.

Tips for Re-teaching:

- Share literature models that provide examples of well-crafted descriptive language, including simile, metaphor, specificity and descriptive attributes.

- Display an object or picture prompt and ask students to write a five-sentence description. Evaluate descriptive language used by the students. Make suggestions for specific types of descriptive devices students can add to their pieces.

- Provide an assortment of prompts and discuss the purpose of each. Provide examples of ways to use descriptive language in different types of writing.

- Isolate skills that are targeted for improvement. Teach these skills explicitly, show samples from literature models, and assign short, concise practice pieces for specific descriptive writing skills.

- Teach skills explicitly and then have students search through literature models to find examples of the specific skills taught.

- Examine drafts of previously written pieces and help students find opportunities to revise these pieces by adding descriptive language.

- Explicitly teach students to read and comprehend questions. Have them restate the question in their own words to check comprehension. Advise students to read all answer choices before selecting a response.

- After re-teaching and independent practice, re-test the students.

"Magic Shoes"

[1] If I had a pair of magic shoes I would want them to fly. [2] I'd soar above my neighborhood and wave to the millions of kids who always spend their afternoons at the playground. [3] They would look up in amazement, with eyes as wide as my grandmother's meatballs! [4] I would give them a friendly wave before turbo-charging my way out of town. [5] I'd fly over the rounded, green hilltops and deep, brown valleys on the outskirts of town. [6] I'd race the cargo train as it hurried along the tracks, trying to reach the station before sundown.

[7] As the sun began to sink lazily behind the shadowy hills, I would drift slowly. [8] I'd turn on my back and wait for the stars to open their eyes and greet me. [9] I'd search for the Big Dipper and Orion's Belt. [10] After circling the pale, white, crescent-shaped moon, I would begin to sink gently back toward the ground. [11] As I settled over my house, I would stop for a moment to gaze at the warm lamp light coming through the windows. [12] The lowered shades would invite me to come in and rest.

[13] If I had a pair of magic shoes, they could take me anywhere, but at the end of the day, I would want them to take me home.

1. Sentence [2] contains which of the following?
    ① Simile
    ② Metaphor
    ③ Personification
    ④ Hyperbole

2. Which sentence uses adverbs to describe how something was done?
    ① Sentence [2]
    ② Sentence [5]
    ③ Sentence [7]
    ④ Sentence [9]

3. Sentence [3] contains which of the following?
    ① Simile
    ② Metaphor
    ③ Personification
    ④ Hyperbole

4. Sentence [6] contains which of the following?
    ① Simile
    ② Metaphor
    ③ Personification
    ④ Hyperbole

5. Sentence [9] contains which of the following?
    ① Simile
    ② Metaphor
    ③ Personification
    ④ Specific details

6. Sentence [10] contains which of the following?
    ① Simile
    ② Metaphor
    ③ Personification
    ④ Descriptive attributes

7. Which of the following sentences contains an example of personification?

    ① Sentence [2]

    ② Sentence [5]

    ③ Sentence [8]

    ④ Sentence [13]

8. Sentence [12] contains which of the following?

    ① Simile

    ② Metaphor

    ③ Personification

    ④ Hyperbole

9. Which of the following sentences does **NOT** contain descriptive attributes?

    ① Sentence [1]

    ② Sentence [5]

    ③ Sentence [7]

    ④ Sentence [10]

10. Which words are used by the author to describe the hills?

    ① Grandmother's meatballs

    ② Rounded, green

    ③ Deep, brown

    ④ Turbo-charging

ASSESSMENT 10, FORM B

Answer Key:

1. ④   2. ③   3. ①   4. ③   5. ④

6. ④   7. ③   8. ③   9. ①   10. ②

Read this piece and answer the questions that follow:

"Rain and More Rain"

[1] Slosh, slosh, slosh. [2] That's all you hear around my neighborhood. [3] We've had so much rain that the ground has turned to mud!

[4] About a month ago, we were all wishing for rain. [5] The lake was drying up and the playground dirt was dry and hard. [6] Everywhere you looked, dust was rising in the air from the dry ground. [7] Then our wish came true. [8] It rained! [9] We were delighted. [10] For three days, it just poured and everyone was happy. [11] Then, on the fourth day, we started to get a little tired of the rain. [12] The dry ground had turned to mud. [13] Raindrops made brown splashes as they hit puddles of water on the ground.

[14] We've had three straight weeks of rainy days now. [15] When will it end? [16] The weather forecasters are predicting rain for the next five days. [17] There is no end in sight. [18] My baseball team keeps practicing in the rain. [19] You should see the tidal wave created by a good slide into second base! [20] My mom suggested, "You boys should change your team colors to match the mud all over our pants!" [21] Yesterday our practice was canceled because of squalls, which were really bad winds that came with the rain. [22] Today we'll be back in the mud again, getting ready to open our season.

[22] Our first game will be held on Saturday. [23] Remember to bring an umbrella if you come to the game. [24] The weatherman is predicting rain!

1. Sentence [1] is a:
    ① Compound sentence
    ② Complex sentence
    ③ Run-on sentence used purposely by the author
    ④ Fragment used purposely by the author

2. Sentence [3] is which of the following?
    ① An interrogative sentence
    ② An exclamatory sentence
    ③ An imperative sentence
    ④ A declarative sentence

3. Sentence [5] is which of the following?
    ① Compound sentence
    ② Complex sentence
    ③ Run-on sentence used purposely by the author
    ④ Fragment used purposely by the author

4. Sentence [6] is a:
    ① Compound sentence
    ② Complex sentence
    ③ Run-on sentence used purposely by the author
    ④ Fragment used purposely by the author

5. Sentence [12] is which of the following?
    ① An interrogative sentence
    ② An exclamatory sentence
    ③ An imperative sentence
    ④ A declarative sentence

6. Sentence [15] is which of the following?

    ① An interrogative sentence

    ② An exclamatory sentence

    ③ An imperative sentence

    ④ A declarative sentence

7. Sentence [20] contains:

    ① A line of dialogue

    ② A definition

    ③ Parentheses

    ④ None of the above

8. Sentence [21] contains:

    ① A line of dialogue

    ② A definition

    ③ Parentheses

    ④ None of the above

9. Sentence [23] is which of the following?

    ① An interrogative sentence

    ② An exclamatory sentence

    ③ An imperative sentence

    ④ A declarative sentence

10. Sentence [24] is which of the following?

    ① An interrogative sentence

    ② An exclamatory sentence

    ③ An imperative sentence

    ④ A declarative sentence

Answer Key:

1. ④	2. ②	3. ①	4. ②	5. ④
6. ①	7. ①	8. ②	9. ③	10. ②

Purpose:

This assessment is designed to evaluate a student's ability to recognize sentence fluency skills. Sentence fluency skills include complex, compound, interrogative, imperative, declarative, and exclamatory sentences, as well as embedded definitions, intentional fragments, and dialogue.

Tips for Re-teaching:

- Share literature models that provide examples of various sentence types, lengths, and structures.

- Offer simple sentences to students and ask them to extend sentences by adding phrases that address where, when, why, and/or how.

- Model and practice combining short, related sentences and segmenting run-on sentences.

- Provide an example of a paragraph with repetitive sentence length and structure. Work with students to revise the paragraph for sentence fluency and variation.

- Provide an assortment of prompts and discuss the purpose of each. Provide examples of ways to use different types of sentences.

- Teach sentence fluency skills explicitly, show samples from literature models, and assign short, concise practice pieces for sentence fluency skills.

- Teach skills explicitly and then have students search through literature models to find examples of the specific skills taught.

- Examine drafts of previously written pieces and help students find opportunities to revise these pieces by varying sentence structures.

- Explicitly teach students to read and comprehend questions. Have them restate the question in their own words to check comprehension. Advise students to read all answer choices before selecting a response.

- After re-teaching and independent practice, re-test the students.

Read this piece and answer the questions that follow:

"A Time of Change"

[1] Colors, temperatures, and back to school. [2] Fall is a time of change.

[3] Have you ever asked yourself which season of the year is the most beautiful? [4] For me, the answer is fall. [5] As temperatures drop, leaves that were once green turn to rich shades of yellow, orange, and red. [6] Deciduous trees – trees that lose their leaves in the winter – provide this wondrous display of color. [7] Mountainsides appear to be painted by the hand of Nature. [8] What a beautiful sight! [9] Scientists would tell us that the leaves are not receiving the nourishment needed to keep their green color. [10] Legends tell us the leaves are splashed with the residue of pre-winter hunting. [11] The reason for the change doesn't really matter to me. [12] It's the beauty of the change that I enjoy.

[13] "Time for school!" I hear Mom shout. [14] After playing through the lazy days of summer, school arrives with schedules and responsibilities. [15] Suddenly the pace picks up. [16] Did I mention homework? [17] After a full day of school, the work continues. [19] In the fall, there is no time for being lazy. [20] You need to wake up to the alarm and you need to stay on task all day.

[21] Colors everywhere, alarms ringing, schools in session, and afternoons filled with homework. [22] Fall is definitely a time of change.

1. Sentence [1] is a:
   ① Fragment used purposely by the author
   ② Run-on sentence used purposely by the author
   ③ Complex sentence
   ④ Compound sentence

2. Sentence [3] is which of the following?
   ① An interrogative sentence
   ② An exclamatory sentence
   ③ An imperative sentence
   ④ A declarative sentence

3. Sentence [6] contains:
   ① A line of dialogue
   ② A definition
   ③ Parentheses
   ④ None of the above

4. Sentence [8] is which of the following?
   ① An interrogative sentence
   ② An exclamatory sentence
   ③ An imperative sentence
   ④ A declarative sentence

5. Sentence [13] contains:
   ① A line of dialogue
   ② A definition
   ③ Parentheses
   ④ None of the above

6. Sentence [14] is which of the following?
   ① Fragment used purposely by the author
   ② Run-on sentence used purposely by the author
   ③ Complex sentence
   ④ Compound sentence

7. Sentence [16] is which of the following?

    ① An interrogative sentence

    ② An exclamatory sentence

    ③ An imperative sentence

    ④ A declarative sentence

8. Sentence [20] contains a:

    ① Fragment used purposely by the author

    ② Run-on sentence used purposely by the author

    ③ Complex sentence

    ④ Compound sentence

9. Sentence [21] is which of the following?

    ① A fragment used purposely by the author

    ② A run-on sentence used purposely by the author

    ③ A complex sentence

    ④ A compound sentence

10. Sentence [22] is which of the following?

    ① An interrogative sentence

    ② An exclamatory sentence

    ③ An imperative sentence

    ④ A declarative sentence

ASSESSMENT 11, FORM B

Answer Key:

1. ①	2. ①	3. ②	4. ②	5. ①
6. ③	7. ①	8. ④	9. ①	10. ④

Chapter Three
Conventions and Mechanics

Language Conventions

Language conventions are the rules of written language. They are generally taught as part of a comprehensive language arts program or within the context of grammar. Written compositions, therefore, become a vehicle for applying these skills rather than a tool for teaching them. There are four main categories of language conventions generally assessed in student writing:

- spelling
- capitalization
- punctuation
- grammar and usage

These skills are not genre-specific. While organization and style vary from genre to genre, the mechanics of writing are consistent. Students master these skills through a combination of explicit instruction, isolated practice, and meaningful application.

Language conventions, when applied correctly, go largely unnoticed. It is only when the writer makes errors in the mechanics of writing that these skills come to the forefront. As part of their education in language conventions, students must be taught to recognize mechanical errors when they occur in a written piece and to proofread and edit their own writing.

Evaluating Language Conventions

Faulty application of language conventions distracts the reader. Good organization, strong vocabulary and well-crafted elements of style all lose their credibility when there are errors in spelling, capitalization, punctuation, grammar and usage.

To diagnose the precise areas of difficulty, multiple-choice assessments are useful tools. Once the areas of difficulty are identified, they can be addressed with re-teaching and practice. Follow-up assessment is then useful in evaluating the effectiveness of the strategies employed.

In conjunction with multiple-choice tests, educators must also teach students to proofread their own pieces. It is generally helpful for students to read their pieces out loud or at least murmur the words to themselves as they proofread. Additionally, students should read a finished piece multiple times, proofreading with a focus on different conventions with each reading.

Assessments

In this section, you will find three kinds of multiple-choice assessments. The first type addresses language conventions in isolation. Students are asked to identify correct and incorrect application of spelling, capitalization, punctuation, grammar and usage.

There are assessments for both basic and advanced language conventions. Basic conventions include spelling of high-frequency words, punctuation, and complete vs. incomplete sentences. Advanced conventions include these skills, taken to a more complex level, in addition to subject-verb agreement, pronoun-antecedent agreement, and consistent tense.

The second type of assessment allows students to practice proofreading skills. Errors in capitalization, punctuation, spelling, grammar and usage are embedded within the context of a written piece. Because language conventions are consistent, the assessments do not need to be genre-specific.

Re-teaching and Re-testing

These assessments follow the same format as earlier chapters. Each skill set is presented in Form A and Form B tests. Form A should be administered as a diagnostic tool. Once scored, the teacher can identify specific language conventions to target for instruction.

Following Form A, you will find an answer key for convenient scoring and a list of suggestions for re-teaching. For further information and reading that can yield additional strategies, a brief bibliography of professional books and a cross-index of literature models are supplied in the Resources.

After re-teaching and practice, administer Form B to determine the effectiveness of the strategies employed. Once again, if a student's performance is flawless on Form A, there is no need for re-teaching and administration of Form B.

Assessments – Conventions and Mechanics

Assessment 12: Language Conventions, Basic

> Form A
>
> Form B

Assessment 13: Language Conventions, Advanced

> Form A
>
> Form B

Assessment 14: Proofreading a Written Piece, Basic

> Form A
>
> Form B

Assessment 15: Proofreading a Written Piece, Advanced

> Form A
>
> Form B

Select the best answer for each question.

1. Which sentence contains correct punctuation?

    ① "Where are you going? she asked."

    ② Where are you going? she asked.

    ③ "Where are you going?" she asked.

    ④ "Where are you going," she asked?

2. Select the complete sentence.

    ① As the sun was sinking beneath the horizon.

    ② When we looked toward the horizon, we saw the sinking sun.

    ③ When we looked toward the horizon, seeing the sinking sun.

    ④ Before we knew it, as the sun was sinking beneath the horizon.

3. In which sentence is every word spelled correctly?

    ① The boys whent to see the school play.

    ② Thay had already purchased their tickets.

    ③ There was a short piano concert before the play.

    ④ The concert began just as they found they're seats.

4. Which sentence contains correct capitalization?

    ① Mrs. Smith is a fantastic Principal.

    ② She works to make Jefferson elementary school great.

    ③ Our School is a place where every student loves to learn.

    ④ Jefferson Elementary School is the best school ever!

5. Which sentence contains correct punctuation?

    ① Where are the books we collected for the hospital.

    ② Did you see Mr. Brown carrying them to his car?

    ③ He is taking them to the hospital for children to read?

    ④ Do you think the children will enjoy reading them!

6. Select the complete sentence.

① My dog learned many tricks at obedience school.

② When I whistle, and he hears the high-pitched sound.

③ As I walk along the sidewalk, carrying his leash in my hand.

④ Whether you have a small dog or a large one.

7. In which sentence is every word spelled correctly?

① The frist thing you must do is read the directions.

② After that, gather all of you're ingredients.

③ You need to make shur you aren't missing any ingredients.

④ Finally, you're ready to start baking!

8. Which sentence contains correct capitalization?

① In Green Bay, Wisconsin, winters are very cold.

② Hawaii is known for its pleasant Climate.

③ As you travel South, you usually find warmer weather.

④ During the Summer, you might miss those cold days!

9. Which sentence contains correct punctuation?

① My big, black, cat is hard to see at night.

② Mrs. Smith has a small, brown dog.

③ I always wanted a large, fierce dog?

④ Instead, I have a, sneaky, furry cat.

10. Select the complete sentence.

① Friends are loyal and trustworthy.

② Because good friends are hard to find.

③ Whenever a friend tells you a secret.

④ If you know how to be a friend.

ASSESSMENT 12, FORM A

Answer Key:

1. ③	2. ②	3. ③	4. ④	5. ②
6. ①	7. ④	8. ①	9. ②	10. ①

Purpose:

This assessment is designed to evaluate a student's ability to recognize correctly applied conventions on a basic level. Conventions include spelling of high-frequency words, punctuation and complete sentences.

Tips for Re-teaching:

- Read samples of the student's writing and identify common error patterns. If the student's error patterns are aligned with errors on this assessment, focus instruction on these specific conventions. If the student's error patterns are not aligned with errors on this assessment, focus on test-taking strategies.

- For spelling, assess the student's mastery of high-frequency words. Select three words at a time to practice, providing mnemonic devices, repeated practice, and "seek and edit missions" in formerly written papers. To seek and edit, the student will search for the selected three words throughout previously written pieces and correct misspellings as they are found.

- For punctuation, isolate the specific errors, re-teach applicable punctuation rules, and allow the student to identify multiple examples of these conventions as they are used in literature models.

- For complete sentences, re-teach simple sentences, identify subjects and predicates, and teach students to "edit by ear," reading sentences aloud to hear the difference between complete and incomplete sentences.

- Explicitly teach students to read all answer choices slowly, "hearing" each choice in their minds.

- After re-teaching and independent practice, re-test the students.

Select the best answer for each question.

1. Which sentence contains correct punctuation?
    ① "Please come in," said Mr. Smith.
    ② "Please come in", said Mr. Smith.
    ③ "Please come in, said Mrs. Smith."
    ④ "Please come in" said Mr. Smith.

2. Select the complete sentence.
    ① Frogs, newts and salamanders.
    ② Because they are amphibians.
    ③ Frogs are common amphibians.
    ④ As you know, and can clearly see.

3. In which sentence is every word spelled correctly?
    ① Please sit with my freind and me.
    ② Do you no the time?
    ③ There were many guests at the party.
    ④ I'm glad that Ben came whith us.

4. Which sentence contains correct capitalization?
    ① My neighbor was born in New York, New York.
    ② Billings, montana is a fascinating place to visit.
    ③ The beaches of florida are popular vacation spots.
    ④ Southern California has a warm Weather.

5. Which sentence contains correct punctuation?
    ① How excited we were to meet our new teacher?
    ② How, excited we were, to meet our new teacher.
    ③ How excited we were to meet our new teacher!
    ④ How, excited we were, to meet our new teacher!

6. Select the complete sentence.

   ① As we walked home after the program, the brisk evening air.

   ② The brisk evening air that followed the program.

   ③ The program, after which we walked home, brisk evening air.

   ④ After the program, we walked home in the brisk, evening air.

7. In which sentence is every word spelled correctly?

   ① I did not know what I should where to the event.

   ② Were do you think we will eat dinner?

   ③ I do not know when were going to arrive.

   ④ Where is your ticket to the show?

8. Which sentence contains correct capitalization?

   ① Frank and Keesha sang in the Fall program.

   ② Each June, Parents and Students plan activities.

   ③ School begins in August, after the Summer break.

   ④ The month of March ushers in a new spring.

9. Which sentence contains correct punctuation?

   ① My favorite colors are green yellow and blue.

   ② We have two dogs, and one cat in our house.

   ③ Did you receive a mysterious, brown envelope?

   ④ I lost a small blue, and white striped package.

10. Select the complete sentence.

   ① Suddenly, the lights flickered and the audience was silent.

   ② Suddenly, and without warning, as we sat quietly.

   ③ Before we knew it as the show was beginning.

   ④ As we waited quietly, suddenly and without warning.

ASSESSMENT 12, FORM B

Answer Key:

1. ①   2. ③   3. ③   4. ①   5. ③

6. ④   7. ④   8. ④   9. ③   10. ①

PURPOSEFUL WRITING ASSESSMENT

Select the best answer for each question.

1. Which sentence does **NOT** contain subject-verb agreement?
   ① The roaring car engines are signaling the start of the race.
   ② He is listening to the radio and ignoring the commotion.
   ③ She says she have a copy of the newspaper article.
   ④ We are leaving for the game at 6:00.

2. Select the complete sentence.
   ① The door opened, no one was there.
   ② She realized she had lost her keys, and she began to retrace her steps.
   ③ He looked around the room, he knew he had spotted her.
   ④ Mara presented her speech, she did a great job.

3. Which sentence contains pronoun-antecedent agreement?
   ① Bring your books to the library and return it to the media specialist.
   ② Each child received a folder, so check them carefully.
   ③ Every girl received a new uniform and must keep them clean.
   ④ The children brought gifts and will exchange them at the party.

4. Which sentence contains consistent tense?
   ① I open the door and shouted with excitement.
   ② She worked for the bank and drives her car there each day.
   ③ As the dog trembled with fear, he reaches to pet it reassuringly.
   ④ They shouted with pride and excitement when he entered the room.

5. Which sentence contains correct spelling **AND** punctuation?
   ① "Have you heard the latest news, she asked excitedly?"
   ② "Wipe the mud from your feet," Mom advised.
   ③ "Have you heard the latest news?" she asked exitedly.
   ④ "Wipe the mud from your feet," Mom adviced.

6. Select the complete sentence.

   ① Wash your clothes with care, you will keep them a long time.

   ② Dan paused in fear for a moment, but he quickly regained his nerve.

   ③ She listens to the radio, he watches television.

   ④ The dog barks loudly, the cat runs to hide.

7. Which sentence contains subject-verb agreement?

   ① Dad went to several stores because he wanted to find the perfect gift.

   ② She speaks three languages and want to teach us some helpful phrases.

   ③ The boys in the blue car is looking this way.

   ④ His daughter like being the belle of the ball.

8. Which sentence contains correct spelling **AND** capitalization?

   ① His mother always makes alot of scrumptious desserts for the bake sale.

   ② Her Dad did not recieve a newsletter in the mail.

   ③ His Mother always makes a lot of scrumptious desserts for the bake sale.

   ④ Her dad did not receive a newsletter in the mail.

9. Which sentence contains pronoun-antecedent agreement?

   ① The children like our new playground, and they visit it frequently.

   ② Mrs. Smith lives close to the fairgrounds, and they don't like the loud noise.

   ③ Parents will receive copies of your tests, and they should review it carefully.

   ④ That new book is fascinating, so put them out on display.

10. Which sentence does **NOT** contain consistent tense?

   ① I told them I was allergic to shellfish, but they must have forgotten.

   ② I search each room meticulously but had not seen the cat.

   ③ She is waking up just now and will return your call very soon.

   ④ If they hadn't heard his cries, they would not have been able to rescue him.

Answer Key:

1. ③	2. ②	3. ④	4. ④	5. ②
6. ②	7. ①	8. ④	9. ①	10. ②

Purpose:

This assessment is designed to evaluate a student's ability to recognize correctly applied conventions on an advanced level. Conventions include spelling of high-frequency words, punctuation, capitalization, complete sentences, subject-verb agreement and pronoun-antecedent agreement.

Tips for Re-teaching:

- Read samples of the student's writing and identify common error patterns. If the student's error patterns are aligned with errors on this assessment, focus instruction on these specific conventions. If the student's error patterns are not aligned with errors on this assessment, focus on test-taking strategies.

- For spelling, assess the student's mastery of high-frequency words. Select three words at a time to practice, providing mnemonic devices, repeated practice, and "seek and edit missions" in formerly written papers. To seek and edit, the student will search for the selected three words throughout previously written pieces and correct misspellings as they are found.

- For punctuation, isolate the specific errors, re-teach applicable punctuation rules, and allow the student to identify multiple examples of these conventions as they are used in literature models.

- For complete sentences, re-teach complex and compound sentences, address independent clauses and coordinating conjunctions, and teach students to "edit by ear," reading sentences aloud to hear the difference between complete and incomplete sentences.

- For pronoun-antecedent agreement, teach students to identify nouns and pronouns in sentences and to isolate these parts of speech to check for consistency.

- For subject-verb agreement, teach students to identify nouns and verbs in sentences and to isolate these parts of speech to check for consistency.

- Explicitly teach students to read all answer choices slowly, "hearing" each choice in their minds.

- After re-teaching and independent practice, re-test the students.

Select the best answer for each question.

1. Which sentence does **NOT** contain subject-verb agreement?

   ① The young ducklings are following close behind their mother.

   ② The students and the teacher was listening carefully to the principal.

   ③ Sam, Joey and Maria are on my team.

   ④ They are preparing for the stormy weather that is headed this way.

2. Which of the following is **NOT** a complete sentence?

   ① She tiptoed carefully past the sleeping dragon.

   ② The cars crept slowly along the highway like snails on pavement.

   ③ As the curious professor searched for information in his numerous books.

   ④ While Josh planned his next move, his opponent stared anxiously.

3. Which sentence contains pronoun-antecedent agreement?

   ① My mother works nearby, so she should be here soon.

   ② Every child has a unique gift and it is our job to find them.

   ③ Your grades are very important, so try to improve it.

   ④ My homework is finished, so I will put them in my backpack.

4. Which sentence contains consistent tense?

   ① I rode my bike on the trail and look at the natural beauty.

   ② They asked the waitress for water and she brings it right away.

   ③ The books are falling from the shelves and she ran out of the way.

   ④ My phone rang and I dropped the book I was reading.

5. Which sentence contains correct spelling **AND** punctuation?

   ① Can you beleive that we are going to be finalists in the competition.

   ② My sister applied for a job at her favorite shopping mall.

   ③ We will be eating in a few minuts, so we shoud wash our hands.

   ④ The coach spoak to the team at half time?

6. Select the complete sentence.

    ① Although we ran quickly and tried to make it on time.

    ② The beauty of the multi-colored rainbow against the morning sky.

    ③ He chased the dog, caught him in the neighbor's yard.

    ④ On each desk, we found a small gift from the teacher.

7. Which sentence does **NOT** contain subject-verb agreement?

    ① Sarah and Jacobie were playing on the same soccer team.

    ② The whole basketball team were celebrating on the court.

    ③ The myriad stars were shining like diamonds in the sky.

    ④ My grandfather's sister was a member of that organization.

8. Which sentence contains correct spelling **AND** capitalization?

    ① Alot of Florida tourists enjoy visiting Key West.

    ② Visitors to South Dakota like to put Mount Rushmore on there agendas.

    ③ A lot of Florida tourists enjoy visiting Key West.

    ④ Visitors to south Dakota like to put mount Rushmore on their agendas.

9. Which sentence contains pronoun-antecedent agreement?

    ① The boys chased him across the field as he carried the ball in his arms.

    ② Mr. Johnson has a truck, and he offered to carry our new trees in them.

    ③ Your assignments are written on the board, and you should copy it down.

    ④ Sisters can be our best friends, so treat her kindly.

10. Which sentence contains consistent tense?

    ① I was reading the directions and take notes on the important details.

    ② Abraham Lincoln makes many speeches that inspired other leaders.

    ③ She is speaking to the principal while we waited in the office.

    ④ We looked in the attic and found his box of old books.

Assessment 13, Form B

Answer Key:

1. ②   2. ③   3. ①   4. ④   5. ②

6. ④   7. ②   8. ③   9. ①   10. ④

Read this piece and answer the questions that follow.

"The Duckbill Platypus"

[1] The duckbill platypus just might be the strangest animal in existence today. [2] Unless you happen to find one in a zoo, the only way you'll see a real, live duckbill platypus is to visit australia. [3] This Australian mammal lives in the water. [4] And swims with its powerful back feet. [5] People who see these strange animals often say, Look at that furry duck! [6] They have wide flat orange bills like a duck. [7] But they have fur instead of feathers. [8] Unlike other mammal's, the platypus lays eggs. [9] Its front feet are strong digging machines. [10] The duckbill platypus is definately an unusual animal!

---

1. Sentence [1]:
   ① Is not a complete sentence.
   ② Needs quotation marks.
   ③ Needs to be indented.
   ④ Contains a misspelled word.

2. In sentence [2]:
   ① A proper noun needs to be capitalized.
   ② The end mark should be changed to a question mark.
   ③ Two words are misspelled.
   ④ No changes are needed.

3. In sentence [3]:
   ① A common noun is incorrectly capitalized.
   ② Quotation marks are needed.
   ③ A word is misspelled.
   ④ No changes are needed.

4. Sentence [4]:
    ① Is not a complete sentence.   ③ Needs to be indented.
    ② Needs quotation marks.   ④ Is correct as written.

5. Sentence [5]:
    ① Is missing commas in a series.   ③ Contains a misspelled word.
    ② Needs quotation marks.   ④ Is correct as written.

6. Sentence [6]:
    ① Is missing commas in a series.   ③ Contains a misspelled word.
    ② Needs quotation marks.   ④ Is correct as written.

7. Sentence [7]:
    ① Is not a complete sentence.   ③ Needs to be indented.
    ② Needs quotation marks.   ④ Is correct as written.

8. In sentence [8]:
    ① An apostrophe should be removed. ③ The end mark should be changed.
    ② A word should be capitalized.   ④ No changes are needed.

9. In sentence [9]:
    ① An apostrophe is needed.   ③ The end mark should be changed.
    ② A word should be capitalized.   ④ No changes are needed.

10. In sentence [10]:
    ① An apostrophe is needed.   ③ A word is misspelled.
    ② A word should be capitalized.   ④ No changes are needed.

ASSESSMENT 14, FORM A

Answer Key:

1. ③	2. ①	3. ④	4. ①	5. ②
6. ①	7. ①	8. ①	9. ④	10. ③

Purpose:

This assessment is designed to evaluate a student's ability to recognize correctly applied conventions on a basic level. Conventions include spelling of high-frequency words, punctuation and complete sentences.

Tips for Re-teaching:

- Read samples of the student's writing and identify common error patterns. If the student's error patterns are aligned with errors on this assessment, focus instruction on these specific conventions. If the student's error patterns are not aligned with errors on this assessment, focus on test-taking strategies.

- For spelling, assess the student's mastery of high-frequency words. Select three words at a time to practice, providing mnemonic devices, repeated practice, and "seek and edit missions" in formerly written papers. To seek and edit, the student will search for the selected three words throughout previously written pieces and correct misspelling as they are found.

- For punctuation, isolate the specific errors, re-teach applicable punctuation rules, and allow the student to identify multiple examples of these conventions as they are used in literature models.

- For complete sentences, re-teach simple sentences, identify subjects and predicates, and teach students to "edit by ear," reading sentences aloud to hear the difference between complete and incomplete sentences.

- Explicitly teach students to read all answer choices slowly, "hearing" each choice in their minds.

- After re-teaching and independent practice, re-test the students.

Read this piece and answer the questions that follow.

"Movie Night"

[1] My family likes to go to the movies. [2] Every week we look in the Newspaper to see what movies are playing. [3] Our favorit theater is the Town Cinema. [4] My parents usually pick out to or three movies. [5] Then my dad says, Okay kids, take your pick. [6] Can you believe that my brother and I sometimes have to flip a coin to make our choice. [7] Or do rock, paper, scissors. [8] Once we decide on a movie, it's off we go! [9] While were riding along, we discuss what we think will happen in the movie. [10] Friday nights are my favorite time of the week!

1. Sentence [1]:
   ① Should not be indented.
   ② Needs a different end mark.
   ③ Needs a capital letter on a proper noun.
   ④ Is correct as written.

2. In sentence [2]:
   ① A common noun is incorrectly capitalized.
   ② Quotation marks are needed.
   ③ A word is misspelled.
   ④ No changes are needed.

3. In sentence [3]:
   ① A common noun is incorrectly capitalized.
   ② Quotation marks are needed.
   ③ A word is misspelled.
   ④ No changes are needed.

4. In sentence [4]:
   ① A proper noun needs to be capitalized.   ③ A word is misspelled.
   ② Quotation marks are needed.   ④ No changes are needed.

5. Sentence [5]:
   ① Is missing commas in a series.   ③ Needs a different end mark.
   ② Needs quotation marks.   ④ Is correct as written.

6. Sentence [6]:
   ① Is missing commas in a series.   ③ Needs a different end mark.
   ② Needs quotation marks.   ④ Is correct as written.

7. Sentence [7]:
   ① Is not a complete sentence.   ③ Needs to be indented.
   ② Needs quotation marks.   ④ Is correct as written.

8. In sentence [8]:
   ① An apostrophe should be removed.   ③ The end mark should be changed.
   ② A word should be capitalized.   ④ No changes are needed.

9. In sentence [9]:
   ① An apostrophe is needed.   ③ The end mark should be changed.
   ② A word should be capitalized.   ④ No changes are needed.

10. In sentence [10]:
    ① An apostrophe is needed.   ③ A word is misspelled.
    ② A word should be capitalized.   ④ No changes are needed.

ASSESSMENT 14, FORM B

Answer Key:

1. ④	2. ①	3. ③	4. ③	5. ②
6. ③	7. ①	8. ④	9. ①	10. ④

Read this piece and answer the questions that follow:

---

[1] Summer is almost here! [2] I'm looking forward to no school family vacation and summer baseball. [3] This summer will be my very best summer ever!

[4] As soon as school is out, my family are leaving for a great vacation. [5] We will drive all the way to south dakota. [6] Well tour Mount Rushmore National Historic Site. [7] My parents plan to take alot of pictures. [8] My brothers, who all want to see the giant heads of presidents. [9] My dad wants to watch a film about Mount Rushmore. [10] My dad is a sculptor and they're interested in the way this giant sculpture was made.

[11] After our vacation, we will come home and start summer baseball. [12] The boys who played on my team this season is all going to return for summer ball. [13] The coach is going to be different, but we heard they will be great. [14] Baseball will be lots of fun.

[15] I can't wait for summer to begin. [16] With vacation and baseball, this will be the best summer ever.

---

1. Sentence [1]:
    ① Should not be indented.
    ② Needs a different end mark.
    ③ Needs capitalization on a proper noun.
    ④ Is correct as written.

2. Sentence [2]:
    ① Needs commas in a series.
    ② Needs a different verb.
    ③ Needs a different pronoun.
    ④ Is correct as written.

3. Sentence [4]:

   ① Needs commas in a series.   ③ Needs a different pronoun.

   ② Needs a different verb.   ④ Is correct as written.

4. Sentence [5]:

   ① Needs a different verb.   ③ Needs capitalization on a proper noun.

   ② Needs a different end mark.   ④ Is correct as written.

5. Sentence [6]:

   ① Needs a different verb.   ③ Needs an apostrophe.

   ② Needs a different pronoun.   ④ Is correct as written.

6. Sentence [7]:

   ① Needs a different verb.   ③ Contains a misspelled word.

   ② Needs a different pronoun.   ④ Is correct as written.

7. Sentence [8]:

   ① Needs a different verb.   ③ Is not a complete sentence.

   ② Needs a different pronoun.   ④ Is correct as written.

8. Sentence [10]:

   ① Needs a different verb.   ③ Is not a complete sentence.

   ② Needs a different pronoun.   ④ Is correct as written.

9. Sentence [12]:

   ① Needs commas in a series.   ③ Needs a different pronoun.

   ② Needs a different verb.   ④ Is correct as written.

10. Sentence [13]:

   ① Needs commas in a series.   ③ Needs a different pronoun.

   ② Needs a different verb.   ④ Is correct as written.

ASSESSMENT 15, FORM A

Answer Key:

1. ④	2. ①	3. ②	4. ③	5. ③
6. ③	7. ③	8. ②	9. ②	10. ③

Purpose:

This assessment is designed to evaluate a student's ability to recognize correctly applied conventions on an advanced level. Conventions include spelling of high-frequency words, punctuation, capitalization, complete sentences, subject-verb agreement and pronoun-antecedent agreement.

Tips for Re-teaching:

- Read samples of the student's writing and identify common error patterns. If the student's error patterns are aligned with errors on this assessment, focus instruction on these specific conventions. If the student's error patterns are not aligned with errors on this assessment, focus on test-taking strategies.

- For spelling, assess the student's mastery of high-frequency words. Select three words at a time to practice, providing mnemonic devices, repeated practice, and "seek and edit missions" in formerly written papers. To seek and edit, the student will search for the selected three words throughout previously written pieces and correct misspellings as they are found.

- For punctuation, isolate the specific errors, re-teach applicable punctuation rules, and allow the student to identify multiple examples of these conventions as they are used in literature models.

- For complete sentences, re-teach complex and compound sentences, address independent clauses and coordinating conjunctions, and teach students to "edit by ear," reading sentences aloud to hear the difference between complete and incomplete sentences.

- For pronoun-antecedent agreement, teach students to identify nouns and pronouns in sentences and to isolate these parts of speech to check for consistency.

- For subject-verb agreement, teach students to identify nouns and verbs in sentences and to isolate these parts of speech to check for consistency.

- Explicitly teach students to read all answer choices slowly, "hearing" each choice in their minds.

- After re-teaching and independent practice, re-test the students.

Read this piece and answer the questions that follow:

[1] Ding, ding! [2] The lonely train whistle blew in the distance as sidney tossed and turned in his old, creaky bed. [3] The clock read midnight and the houses all along his street is quiet.

[4] Every night at midnight, he has the same problem. [5] Sidney wakes up to the train whistle and he couldn't go back to sleep. [6] Sidney had tried many ways to solve his problem. [7] First, he wore earplugs to bed. [8] He didn't here the train whistle. [9] But he slept right through his alarm the next morning. [10] Next, he put heavy curtains on his window, but it didn't block the sound.

[11] Finally, he found the perfect solution. [12] Sidney bought a tape of soothing sounds. [13] Such as whale songs and cello music. [14] He plays the tape all night long. [15] Now when the train comes by, it sounds like whale songs cello music or some other soothing sound.

[16] Ding, ding. [17] The lonely train whistle still blow in the distance, but Sidney goes right on sleeping.

1. Sentence [2]:
   ① Should not be indented.
   ② Needs a different end mark.
   ③ Needs capitalization on a proper noun.
   ④ Is correct as written.

2. Sentence [3]:
   ① Needs a different verb.
   ② Needs a different pronoun.
   ③ Needs an apostrophe.
   ④ Is correct as written.

3. Sentence [4]:
   ① Needs commas in a series.
   ② Needs a different end mark.
   ③ Needs capitalization on a proper noun.
   ④ Is correct as written.

4. Sentence [5]:
   ① Needs a different verb.
   ② Needs a different pronoun.
   ③ Needs an apostrophe.
   ④ Is correct as written.

5. Sentence [8]:
   ① Needs a different verb.
   ② Needs a different pronoun.
   ③ Contains a misspelled word.
   ④ Is correct as written.

6. Sentence [9]:
   ① Needs a different verb.
   ② Needs a different pronoun.
   ③ Is not a complete sentence.
   ④ Is correct as written.

7. Sentence [10]:
   ① Needs a different verb.
   ② Needs a different pronoun.
   ③ Contains a misspelled word.
   ④ Is correct as written.

8. Sentence [13]:
   ① Needs a different verb.
   ② Needs a different pronoun.
   ③ Is not a complete sentence.
   ④ Is correct as written.

9. Sentence [15]:
   ① Needs commas in a series.
   ② Needs a different end mark.
   ③ Needs capitalization on a proper noun.
   ④ Is correct as written.

10. Sentence [17]:
    ① Needs a different verb.
    ② Needs a different pronoun.
    ③ Is not a complete sentence.
    ④ Is correct as written.

ASSESSMENT 15, FORM B

Answer Key:

1. ③	2. ①	3. ④	4. ①	5. ③
6. ③	7. ②	8. ③	9. ①	10. ①

Resources

Jana created this plan to help her organize her ideas before writing. Read her plan and then answer the questions that follow.

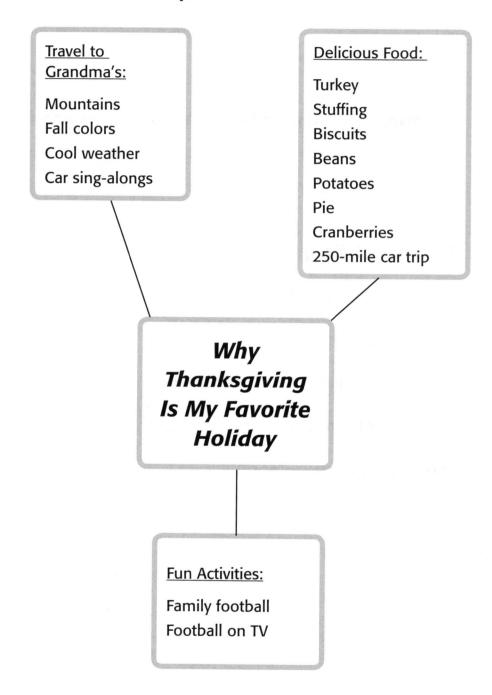

Travel to Grandma's:

Mountains
Fall colors
Cool weather
Car sing-alongs

Delicious Food:

Turkey
Stuffing
Biscuits
Beans
Potatoes
Pie
Cranberries
250-mile car trip

Why Thanksgiving Is My Favorite Holiday

Fun Activities:

Family football
Football on TV

1. What kind of paper is Jana planning to write?
   ① Expository
   ② Narrative
   ③ Comparison
   ④ Persuasive

2. What is the topic of Jana's paper?
   ① Travel to Grandma's
   ② Delicious Food
   ③ Fun Activities
   ④ My Favorite Holiday

3. Jana wants to add "cornbread" to her plan. In which box should she add this new detail?
   ① Travel to Grandma's
   ② Delicious Food
   ③ Fun Activities
   ④ None of the above

4. Which sub-topic seems to be the weakest and should probably become the middle body paragraph?
   ① Travel to Grandma's
   ② Delicious Food
   ③ Fun Activities
   ④ None of the above

5. Which detail is out of place and should be moved?
   ① Cool weather
   ② 250-mile car trip
   ③ Family football
   ④ None of the above

Michael was asked to write a story about his favorite memory. This is Michael's plan:

> ## My special memory:
>
> October:
>
> - -saw an electric guitar in store
> - -begged parents to get it
>
> November:
>
> - -offered to do jobs around the house
> - -no guitar
>
> December:
>
> - -kept begging
> - -Mom said I was only getting shoes for Christmas
> - -Christmas morning, big package
> - -got guitar

Answer the following questions about Michael's plan:

6. What type of paper is Michael planning to write?
    - ① Expository
    - ② Narrative
    - ③ Comparison
    - ④ Persuasive

7. What type of plan did Michael create to help him organize his ideas?
    - ① Timeline
    - ② Venn diagram
    - ③ Storyboard
    - ④ Web

This is Michael's rough draft about his special memory:

My Special Memory

[1] I saw a metallic-blue electric guitar in the display window of a store. [2] I couldn't take my eyes off of it. [3] It was long and thin. [4]It had shiny, silver sparkles. [5] A rectangular, white tag dangled from the neck of the guitar. [6] It said, "For Sale: $150.00."

[7] I asked my parents if they would get it for me. [8] They just shook their heads and said it cost too much money. [9] I begged and begged, but they didn't change their minds.

[10] After a few weeks of thinking, I made a plan. [11] I thought that I could earn the money to buy the guitar for myself if only I could find some jobs to do. [12] I talked to my dad about mowing the lawn and washing the car. [13] He said he would like to have my help, but he would not pay more than twenty dollars for both jobs.

[14] Soon I had another idea. [15] Christmas was just around the corner. [16] I asked my mom if I could get the guitar for Christmas. [17] She reminded me that I had already asked for new basketball shoes that were very expensive. [18] My guitar dream seemed hopeless.

[19] On Christmas morning, I walked into the living room and saw a long, narrow package leaning against the wall next to the tree. [20] I tore through the paper in a hurry. [21] Inside, I found the shiny, blue-metallic guitar. [22] My parent just smiled. [23] It was the best Christmas ever, and the memory of that day always brings a smile to my face.

8. Which of the following sentences should be added before sentence [1] to gain the reader's interest and introduce the topic?

① Hello, my name is Michael.

② I am going to tell you a story about my special day.

③ Of all my special memories, there is one that I treasure most.

④ Do you have a guitar?

9. Read these two sentences from Michael's story:

[3] It was long and thin. [4] It had shiny, silver sparkles.

Michael wants to change these sentences. What would be the best choice for revising these two sentences?

① Divide them into three or four shorter sentences.

② Remove these sentences from the story.

③ Combine these two sentences to make one new sentence.

④ Leave these sentences as they are written.

10. Which of the following sentences contains a strong verb?

① Sentence [3]

② Sentence [5]

③ Sentence [6]

④ Sentence [14]

11. Michael would like to add this line of dialogue:

My dad said, "Michael, you'll just have to take NO for an answer."

Where should Michael add this line of dialogue?

① After sentence [1]

② After sentence [7]

③ After sentence [9]

④ After sentence [15]

12. Why is sentence [6] an effective sentence?

① It is in Michael's plan.

② It provides a specific detail about the guitar.

③ It explains why the guitar is important to Michael.

④ It is not effective and should be removed.

13. Which of the following sentences contains descriptive language?

① Sentence [9]

② Sentence [14]

③ Sentence [16]

④ Sentence [19]

The paper below is a rough draft of a report written by Grace. Her teacher asked her to revise and edit her paper. Read Grace's rough draft and answer the questions that follow.

Three Cheers for Recycling

[1] How do you get rid of 64 million tons of garbage without throwing it away? [2] The answer is: you recycle it. [3] In 1999, americans recycled 64 million tons of waste, and since then, recycling has continued to grow.

[4] You can recycle paper products. [5] Most communities have curb side recycling of paper products. [6] If your community does not has this service, then check with your local government to find out where you can find large containers used for collecting items to be recycled.

[7] Some other things you can recycle are plastic and aluminum. [8] Plastic water bottles and aluminum cans that are tossed in the garbage end up in landfills. [9] If you send these items to a landfill, they will probably still be there even after you have grandchildren and your hair is as white as snow on a polar bear.

[10] Finally, you can recycle many electronics. [11] You can check with the store where you bought your computer, digital camera or other electronic device to find out where electronics can be recycled in your community. [12] I have my own computer.

[13] The next time you want to toss some paper, plastic, aluminum or electronics into the trash, consider recycling instead.

14. What type of correction does Grace need to make in sentence [3]?

   ① She needs to make a spelling correction.

   ② Sentence [3] is not a complete sentence.

   ③ She needs to capitalize a proper noun.

   ④ This sentence is correct as it is written.

15. Which of the following would be an effective transition for Grace to add before sentence [4]?

① Last but not least,

② To begin with,

③ Another thing you can recycle,

④ Additionally,

16. Grace wants to add this detail:

It's sad to think that 40% of the garbage in an average landfill is made of paper that could have been recycled.

Where should Grace add this detail?

① After sentence [4]

② After sentence [7]

③ After sentence [10]

④ This detail does not support the topic and should not be added.

17. Which detail does not support the topic and should be omitted?

① Sentence [3]

② Sentence [5]

③ Sentence [8]

④ Sentence [12]

18. Which of the following sentences contains a simile?

① Sentence [3]

② Sentence [6]

③ Sentence [9]

④ Sentence [11]

19. In sentence [6], Grace needs to change which of the following?

① Change "your" to "their"

② Change "has" to "have"

③ Change "this" to "these"

④ This sentence is correct as it is written.

Read "My Family Zoo." Select the word or words that correctly fill in the blanks to answer questions 15-20.

My Family Zoo

Does your family seem a little unusual? Let me tell __[20]__ about my family zoo and your family will probably seem pretty normal.

First of all, there's my dad. He is almost seven feet tall. When he drives, he has to lean forward so that his head __[21]__ touch the car ceiling. He ducks his head when he goes through doorways. He __[22]__ like a nodding ostrich when he walks around our house.

My dad might be tall, but my mom is a shrimp. She loves to cook, but she has to use a stepladder to reach the kitchen cabinets. She is always __[23]__ up and down like a hyperactive parakeet!

Next there's my little sister. Her name is Lark, but she sings more like a cat than a bird. She sings in the shower __[24]__ she sings in the car. She sings wherever we go. Sometimes I just need some peace and quiet, so I put earplugs on my birthday list this year!

My story would not be complete without telling you about me. I am an expert at observing and studying animal behavior. One day I hope to be a zookeeper. My family is helping me prepare for my career!

You might think my family is a little crazy, but I wouldn't trade them for the world. As the saying goes, __[25]__ more fun than a barrel of monkeys!

20. Which word should go in blank [20]?

   ① him

   ② her

   ③ you

   ④ them

21. Which word(s) should go in blank [21]?

    ① wont

    ② won't

    ③ wo'nt

    ④ wount

22. Which word should go in blank [22]?

    ① looking

    ② looked

    ③ look

    ④ looks

23. Which word should go in blank [23]?

    ① climbing

    ② climbed

    ③ climb

    ④ climbs

24. Which word should go in blank [24]?

    ① but

    ② however

    ③ and

    ④ also

25. Which word should go in blank [25]?

    ① they're

    ② their

    ③ there

    ④ None of the above

COMPREHENSIVE WRITING ASSESSMENT, FORM A

Answer Key:

1. ① - focus and organization: purpose for writing
2. ④ - focus and organization: main idea
3. ② - focus and organization: grouping related details
4. ③ - focus and organization: ordering paragraphs
5. ② - focus and organization: grouping related details
6. ② - focus and organization: purpose for writing
7. ① - focus and organization: planning
8. ③ - focus and organization: beginning techniques
9. ③ - style and composition: sentence variation
10. ② - style and composition: strong verbs
11. ③ - style and composition: dialogue
12. ② - style and composition: descriptive language
13. ④ - style and composition: descriptive language
14. ③ - conventions and mechanics: capitalization
15. ② - focus and organization: transitions
16. ① - style and composition: supporting details
17. ④ - style and composition: supporting details
18. ③ - style and composition: descriptive language
19. ② - conventions and mechanics: usage
20. ③ - conventions and mechanics: usage
21. ② - conventions and mechanics: spelling
22. ④ - conventions and mechanics: usage
23. ① - conventions and mechanics: usage
24. ③ - conventions and mechanics: usage
25. ① - conventions and mechanics: spelling

···

Focus and Organization _____ out of 9

Style and Composition _____ out of 8

Conventions and Mechanics _____ out of 8

Comments:

Ricardo created this plan to help him organize his ideas before writing. Read his plan and then answer the questions that follow.

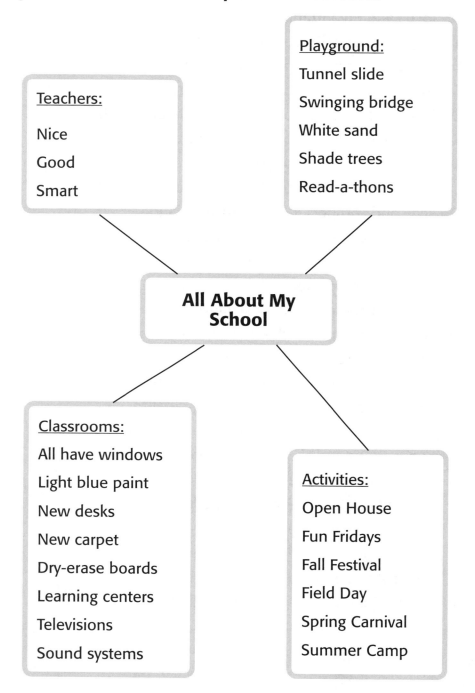

1. What kind of paper is Ricardo planning to write?

    ① Expository

    ② Narrative

    ③ Comparison

    ④ Persuasive

2. What is the purpose of Ricardo's paper?

    ① To inform the reader about his school

    ② To compare his school to other schools in the area

    ③ To describe his school's playground

    ④ To entertain the reader with humorous stories about his teachers

3. Ricardo wants to add "field trips" to his plan. In which box should he add this new detail?

    ① Teachers

    ② Playground

    ③ Activities

    ④ Classrooms

4. Which sub-topic seems to be the weakest and needs to be improved with additional details, deleted, or combined with another sub-topic?

    ① Teachers

    ② Playground

    ③ Activities

    ④ Classrooms

5. Which detail is out of place and should be moved?

    ① Fall Festival

    ② Light blue paint

    ③ Read-a-thons

    ④ None of the above

Marsha was asked to write a story about her funniest memory. This is Marsha's plan:

My funniest memory:

7:30

   ✓woke up late

   ✓got dressed in a hurry (shoes on wrong feet)

8:00

   ✓went to kitchen – mom not around

   ✓hurried and ate a bowl of cereal

8:20

   ✓grabbed backpack, yelled goodbye to mom

   ✓ran to bus stop…waited…worried I missed bus

8:35

   ✓saw my friend, Jessie, on her bike

   ✓she stopped and asked if I wanted to ride with her

   ✓suddenly realized it was Saturday

Answer the following questions about Marsha's plan:

6.   What type of paper is Marsha planning to write?

   ① Informational expository

   ② Personal narrative

   ③ Comparison

   ④ Steps to a process

7.   What type of plan did Marsha create to help him organize his ideas?

   ① Timeline

   ② Venn diagram

   ③ Outline

   ④ Web

This is Marsha's rough draft about her funniest memory:

My Funniest Memory

[1] I am going to tell you about my funniest memory. [2] One morning I woke up and saw the sun coming through the window. [3] My alarm did not ring. [4] I knew I was going to be late for school.

[5] I jumped out of bed and got dressed in a hurry. [6] I put on my comfortable, old, blue jeans and a trusty, gray sweatshirt that was hanging on the back of my desk chair. [7] I slipped my feet into my tennis shoes. [8] I didn't stop to tie the laces. [9] As I raced down the stairs, I realized my shoes were on the wrong feet, but I didn't have time to worry about that.

[10] When I reached the kitchen, I thought it was strange that my mom was nowhere in sight. [11] I called out to her, but there was no answer. [12] I quickly gobbled down a bowl of cereal, grabbed my backpack, and headed for the door. [13] As the door was swinging shut behind me, I yelled, "Bye, Mom!" [14] There was still no answer.

[15] I ran all the way to the bus stop with my shoelaces flopping around on the sidewalk. [16] When I went to my stop, no one was there. [17] I was afraid I had missed my bus, but I decided to wait a few minutes just in case. [18] I felt relieved when I saw my friend Jessie riding her bike toward me. [19] Strangely enough, she was not rushing at all. [20] She called out and asked if I wanted to ride my bike with her. [21] Suddenly, I realized it was Saturday. [22] Jessie and I laughed all the way back to my house. [23] We rode our bikes the rest of the day.

8. Which of the following sentences could replace sentence [1] to make a stronger introduction to Marsha's story?

    ① We all have memories to treasure, but my favorite memory is the one that makes me laugh every time I think about it.

    ② I am going to tell you all about my funny day.

    ③ Most mornings I wake up to my alarm clock ringing, but one day I woke up and my alarm clock wasn't ringing.

    ④ Hi, I'm Marsha.

9. Read these two sentences from Marsha's story:

    [3] I slipped my feet into my tennis shoes. [4] I didn't stop to tie the laces.

    Marsha wants to change these sentences. Which of the following would be the best choice for revising these two sentences?

    ① Make these sentences present tense.

    ② Combine these two sentences to make one sentence.

    ③ Remove them from the story because they are off topic.

    ④ Move these sentences after sentence [1].

10. Which of the following sentences does **NOT** contain a strong verb?

    ① Sentence [7]

    ② Sentence [9]

    ③ Sentence [12]

    ④ Sentence [16]

11. Marsha would like to add this detail:

    I thought this was strange because my mom is usually the first one up at my house.

    Where should Marsha add this detail?

    ① After sentence [1]

    ② After sentence [7]

    ③ After sentence [9]

    ④ After sentence [11]

12. Why is sentence [15] an effective sentence?

① It lets the reader know that the story is finished.

② It lets the reader know what the character is thinking.

③ It helps the reader picture what is happening in the story.

④ It is not effective and should be removed.

13. Which of the following sentences contains descriptive language?

① Sentence [4]

② Sentence [6]

③ Sentence [14]

④ Sentence [17]

The paper below is a rough draft written by Isaac to explain why he thinks science is important. His teacher asked him to revise and edit his paper. Read Isaac's rough draft and answer the questions that follow.

Science

[1] Do you think science is important? [2] Well, I do and I am going to tell you why.

[3] To begin with, science can save lives. [4] Did you know that doctors are scientists? [5] Many generations ago people died from simple injuries and illnesses that can be cured today because of science. [6] Meteorologists are scientists who study weather. [7] Thanks to these scientists, we can predict terrible storms and prepare for them before they arrive. [8] The study of science has also led to many inventions that makes life safer and easier for all of us.

[9] You should also know that science is the study of the world all around us. [10] Without science, we would not be able to understand our Environment, the way things work, or why things happen the way they do. [11] Scientists let us know when some animals are endangered and they study ways to help these animals. [12] My favorite animal is a dog, but my sister likes cats best. [13] Scientists let us know when things we do pollute our planet and can be bad for us. [14] This makes life better for everyone.

[15] Everyone needs to study science. [16] It's the one subject that can save our lives and make our planet a better place to live.

14. What type of correction does Isaac need to make in sentence [10]?
    ① He misspelled a word.
    ② He capitalized a common noun.
    ③ He forgot to capitalize a proper noun.
    ④ This sentence is correct as it is written.

15. Which of the following would be an effective transition for Isaac to add before sentence [3]?

    ① Finally,

    ② First,

    ③ Also,

    ④ Sentence [3] already contains a transition.

16. Isaac wants to add this detail:

    For example, the mystery of the hole in our ozone layer was solved by scientists who discovered that a type of air pollution was the cause!

    Where should Isaac add this detail?

    ① After sentence [7]

    ② After sentence [11]

    ③ After sentence [13]

    ④ This detail does not support the topic and should not be added.

17. Which sentence does not support the topic and should be omitted?

    ① Sentence [4]

    ② Sentence [7]

    ③ Sentence [10]

    ④ Sentence [12]

18. Which of the following sentences contains a definition?

    ① Sentence [3]

    ② Sentence [6]

    ③ Sentence [10]

    ④ Sentence [11]

19. In sentence [8], Grace needs to change which of the following?

    ① Change "makes" to "make"

    ② Change "has" to "have"

    ③ Change "for" to "four"

    ④ This sentence is correct as it is written.

Read "My Hero." Select the word or words that correctly fill in the blanks to answer questions 20-25.

My Hero

Many people have special heroes. I would like to tell you about my hero. I _[20]_ her Mom.

The main reason I look up to my mother is because she can do almost anything. _[21]_ wouldn't believe how smart she is! When I need help with my homework, she is like a walking encyclopedia. It _[22]_ matter if it's math, reading, spelling, history or science – my mom knows it all! She is also like a magician when it comes to putting together a party in no time at all. Once she _[23]_ together a celebration for my whole soccer team in just one day!

Another thing that makes her my hero is that I can always count on my mom. If she says she is going to do something, you know she will do it. One time I was afraid that she had _[24]_ about my class field trip, but when we arrived at the museum, she was there waiting for us. Even when she has a lot on her mind, she never forgets about me. One time she even postponed a business meeting so she could be at my soccer game. I knew she would be _[25]_. My mother is the most dependable person I know.

My mother is smart and dependable. She can do just about anything and she never lets me down. That's why my mother is my hero.

---

20. Which word should go in blank [20]?

    ① calls

    ② called

    ③ call

    ④ calling

21. Which word should go in blank [21]?

    ① You

    ② I

    ③ She

    ④ We

22. Which word should go in blank [22]?

    ① don't

    ② doesn't

    ③ didn't

    ④ couldn't

23. Which word should go in blank [23]?

    ① though

    ② thru

    ③ through

    ④ threw

24. Which word should go in blank [24]?

    ① forget

    ② forgot

    ③ forgotten

    ④ forgetting

25. Which word should go in blank [25]?

    ① they're

    ② their

    ③ there

    ④ none of the above

Answer Key:

1. ① - focus and organization: purpose for writing
2. ① - focus and organization: main idea
3. ③ - focus and organization: grouping related details
4. ① - focus and organization: building paragraphs
5. ③ - focus and organization: grouping related details
6. ② - focus and organization: purpose for writing
7. ① - focus and organization: planning
8. ① - focus and organization: beginning techniques
9. ② - style and composition: sentence variation
10. ④ - style and composition: strong verbs
11. ④ - style and composition: supporting details
12. ③ - style and composition: descriptive language
13. ② - style and composition: descriptive language
14. ② - conventions and mechanics: capitalization
15. ④ - focus and organization: transitions
16. ③ - style and composition: supporting details
17. ④ - style and composition: supporting details
18. ② - style and composition: embedded definitions
19. ① - conventions and mechanics: usage
20. ③ - conventions and mechanics: usage
21. ① - conventions and mechanics: spelling
22. ② - conventions and mechanics: usage
23. ④ - conventions and mechanic: spelling
24. ③ - conventions and mechanics: usage
25. ③ - conventions and mechanics: spelling

....

Focus and Organization _____ out of 9

Style and Composition _____ out of 8

Conventions and Mechanics _____ out of 8

Comments:

Appendix B

Progress Monitoring Tool: Organization and Focus

Assessment 1:

Form A: Date: _____   Score: _____   Comments:

Form B: Date: _____   Score: _____   Comments:

Assessment 2:

Form A: Date: _____   Score: _____   Comments:

Form B: Date: _____   Score: _____   Comments:

Assessment 3:

Form A: Date: _____   Score: _____   Comments:

Form B: Date: _____   Score: _____   Comments:

Assessment 4:

Form A: Date: _____   Score: _____   Comments:

Form B: Date: _____   Score: _____   Comments:

Assessment 5:

Form A: Date: _____   Score: _____   Comments:

Form B: Date: _____   Score: _____   Comments:

Progress Monitoring Tool: Style and Composition

Assessment 6:

Form A: Date: _____   Score: _____   Comments:

Form B: Date: _____   Score: _____   Comments:

Assessment 7:

Form A: Date: _____   Score: _____   Comments:

Form B: Date: _____   Score: _____   Comments:

Assessment 8:

Form A: Date: _____   Score: _____   Comments:

Form B: Date: _____   Score: _____   Comments:

Assessment 9:

Form A: Date: _____   Score: _____   Comments:

Form B: Date: _____   Score: _____   Comments:

Assessment 10:

Form A: Date: _____   Score: _____   Comments:

Form B: Date: _____   Score: _____   Comments:

Assessment 11:

Form A: Date: _____   Score: _____   Comments:

Form B: Date: _____   Score: _____   Comments:

Progress Monitoring Tool: Conventions and Mechanics

Assessment 12:

Form A: Date: _____ Score: _____   Comments:

Form B: Date: _____ Score: _____   Comments:

Assessment 13:

Form A: Date: _____ Score: _____   Comments:

Form B: Date: _____ Score: _____   Comments:

Assessment 14:

Form A: Date: _____ Score: _____   Comments:

Form B: Date: _____ Score: _____   Comments:

Assessment 15:

Form A: Date: _____ Score: _____   Comments:

Form B: Date: _____ Score: _____   Comments:

Assessment 16:

Form A: Date: _____ Score: _____   Comments:

Form B: Date: _____ Score: _____   Comments:

Bibliography of Professional Books

Planning a focused personal narrative piece

Culham, Ruth. *6 + 1 Traits of Writing: The Complete Guide*, New York, NY: Scholastic, 2003.

Forney, Melissa. *Razzle Dazzle Writing*, Gainesville, FL: Maupin House Publishing, 2003.

Freeman, Marcia S. *Building a Writing Community*, Gainesville, FL: Maupin House Publishing, 1995.

Planning a focused fictional narrative piece

Calkins, Lucy. *The Art of Teaching Writing,* Portsmouth, NH: Heinemann, 1986.

Forney, Melissa. *The Writing Menu*, Gainesville, FL: Maupin House Publishing, 1999.

Jorgensen, Karen. *The Whole Story: Crafting Fiction in the Upper Elementary Grades.* Portsmouth, NH: Heinemann, 2001.

Planning a focused expository piece

Freeman, Marcia S. *Building a Writing Community*, Gainesville, FL: Maupin House Publishing, 1995.

Freeman, Marcia S. *Listen to This: Developing an Ear for Expository*, Gainesville, FL: Maupin House Publishing, 1997.

Koehler, Susan. *Crafting Expository Papers,* Gainesville, FL: Maupin House Publishing, 2007.

Focus and organization in a personal narrative piece

Fiderer, Adele. *Mini-Lessons for Teaching Writing.* Jefferson City, MO: Scholastic, 1997.

Freeman, Marcia S. *Building a Writing Community*, Gainesville, FL: Maupin House Publishing, 1995.

Harris, Karen and Steve Graham. *Making the Writing Process Work: Strategies for Compositions and Self-Regulation.* Cambridge, MA: Brookline Books, 1999.

Organizational skills: author's purpose, beginning and ending techniques, transitions, supporting details, and focus

Cole, Ardith Davis. *Better Answers.* Portland, ME: Stenhouse Publishers, 2005.

Harris, Karen and Steve Graham. *Making the Writing Process Work: Strategies for Composition and Self-Regulation.* Cambridge, MA: Brookline Books, 1999.

Koehler, Susan. *Crafting Expository Papers.* Gainesville, FL: Maupin House Publishing, 2007.

Word choice made by an author to create interest and style in a written piece

Carnicelli, Thomas. *Words Work*, Portsmouth, NH: Boynton/Cook Publishers, 2001.

Forney, Melissa. *Razzle Dazzle Writing*, Gainesville, FL: Maupin House Publishing, 2003.

Ray, Katie Wood. *Wondrous Words: Writers and Writing in the Elementary Classroom*,

Urbana, IL: Wood Council Teachers of English, 1999.

Descriptive language and devices used by an author to help the reader visualize text

Atwell, Nancie. *Lessons That Change Writers.* Portsmouth, NH: Heinemann, 2002.

Forney, Melissa. *Razzle Dazzle Writing*, Gainesville, FL: Maupin House Publishing, 2003.

Fountas, Irene C. and Gay Su Pinnell. *Guiding Readers and Writers.* Portsmouth, NH: Heinnemann, 2001.

Sentence fluency

Atwell, Nancie. *Lessons That Change Writers.* Portsmouth, NH: Heinemann, 2002.

Culham, Ruth. *6 + 1 Traits of Writing: The Complete Guide*, New York, NY: Scholastic, 2003.

Koehler, Susan. *Crafting Expository Papers*, Gainesville, FL: Maupin House Publishing, 2007.

Word choice: strong verbs, alliteration, onomatopoeia, transitions, dialogue tags, and pronouns used to address the reader

Carnicelli, Thomas. *Words Work*, Portsmouth, NH: Boynton/Cook Publishing, 2001.

Freeman, Marcia S. *Building a Writing Community*, Gainesville, FL: Maupin House Publishing, 1995.

Ray, Katie Wood. *Wondrous Words: Writers and Writing in the Elementary Classroom*,

Urbana, IL: Wood Council Teachers of English, 1999.

Descriptive attributes (adjectives and adverbs): simile, metaphor, personification, hyperbole, and specificity

Atwell, Nancie. *Lessons That Change Writers.* Portsmouth, NH: Heinemann, 2002.

Fountas, Irene C. and Gay Su Pinnell. *Guiding Readers and Writers.* Portsmouth, NH: Heinnemann, 2001.

Freeman, Marcia S. *Building a Writing Community*, Gainesville, FL: Maupin House Publishing, 1995.

Sentence fluency: complex, compound, interrogative, imperative, declarative, and exclamatory sentences; embedded definitions; intentional fragments; and dialogue

Atwell, Nancie. *Lessons That Change Writers.* Portsmouth, NH: Heinemann, 2002.

Culham, Ruth. *6 + 1 Traits of Writing: The Complete Guide*, New York, NY: Scholastic, 2003.

Koehler, Susan. *Crafting Expository Papers*, Gainesville, FL: Maupin House Publishing, 2007.

Conventions: spelling high-frequency words, punctuation, complete sentences, capitalization, subject-verb agreement, and pronoun-antecedent agreement

Anderson, Jeff. *Mechanically Inclined.* Portland, ME: Stenhouse Publishers, 2005.

Freeman, Marcia S. *Building a Writing Community*, Gainesville, FL: Maupin House Publishing, 1996.

Terban, Marvin. *Scholastic Writer's Desk Reference*, New York, NY: Scholastic, 2000.

Culham, Ruth. *6 + 1 Traits of Writing: The Complete Guide*, New York, NY: Scholastic, 2003.

These models are suggested for the specific skills in this book. You may find that the models apply to more than one skill or that the skills listed work with other models of your choice. You can check off additional skills for the models listed or add your own models to the blank charts provided at the end of this index.

Index of Literature Models

The following skills are listed across the top of the chart (columns):

Dialogue and quotations · Embedded definitions · Exclamations · Simile, metaphor, personification, adjectives, & specificity · Transitions · Pronouns · Dialogue and quotations · Strong verbs, alliteration, and onomatopoeia · Sentence variation · Description · Repetition · Alliteration · Supporting details · Transitions · Endings · Beginnings · Focus & organization in personal narrative · Expository · Fiction plot types · Characters, events, and conflicts · Personal narratives

Title	Author	Checked skills
A. Lincoln and Me	Louise Borden	Dialogue and quotations; Endings
A is for Abigail	Lynne Cherry	
A New Coat for Anna	Harriet Ziefert	Sentence variation
A Pizza the Size of the Sun	Jack Prelutsky	Repetition
Absolutely Normal Chaos	Sharon Creech	Transitions
Africa Dream	Eloise Greenfield	Description
Alexander and the Wind-Up Mouse	Leo Lionni	Endings
All Those Secrets of the World	Jane Yolen	Characters, events, and conflicts
Appalachia: The Voices of Sleeping Birds	Cynthia Rylant	Exclamations; Alliteration
Because of Winn-Dixie	Kate DiCamillo	Fiction plot types
Big Al	Andrew Clements	Transitions; Repetition
Bigmama's	Donald Crews	Dialogue and quotations
Boy	Roald Dahl	Simile, metaphor, personification, adjectives, & specificity; Characters, events, and conflicts
Brave Irene	William Steig	Dialogue and quotations; Sentence variation
Canoe Days	Gary Paulsen	Pronouns
Castle	David Macaulay	
Catfish and Spaghetti	Marcia S. Freeman	Exclamations

Index of Literature Models

Title	Author	Dialogue and quotations	Embedded definitions	Exclamations	Simile, metaphor, personification, adjectives, & specificity	Transitions	Pronouns	Dialogue and quotations	Strong verbs, alliteration, and onomatopoeia	Sentence variation	Description	Repetition	Alliteration	Supporting details	Transitions	Endings	Beginnings	Focus & organization in personal narrative	Expository	Fiction plot types	Characters, events, and conflicts	Personal narratives
Charlotte's Web	E. B. White				✓					✓												
Chrysanthemum	Kevin Henkes	✓															✓					
Clay Hernandez: A Mexican American	Diane Hoyt-Goldsmith											✓							✓			
Click, Clack, Moo: Cows That Type	Doreen Cronin								✓													
Crocodile Tea	Marcia Vaughan								✓													
Crow Boy	Taro Yashima																✓					
Eleanor	Barbara Cooney																		✓			
Emily	Michael Bedard								✓													
Each Little Bird That Sings	Deborah Wiles							✓														
Falling Up	Shel Silverstein															✓						
Fever 1793	Laurie Halse Anderson																✓					
Fireboat: The Heroic Adventures of the John J. Harvey	Maira Kalman																		✓			
Freedom Summer	Deborah Wiles				✓												✓					
Goodbye Geese	Nancy Carlstrom				✓																	
Harry Potter and the Goblet of Fire	J. K. Rowling																					
Harry Potter and the Sorcerer's Stone	J. K. Rowling							✓														
Hey! Get Off Our Train	John Burningham								✓													
How I Became a Pirate	Melinda Long						✓															

Index of Literature Models

Title	Author	Dialogue and quotations	Embedded definitions	Exclamations	Simile, metaphor, personification, adjectives, & specificity	Transitions	Pronouns	Dialogue and quotations	Strong verbs, alliteration, and onomatopoeia	Sentence variation	Description	Repetition	Alliteration	Supporting details	Transitions	Endings	Beginnings	Focus & organization in personal narrative	Expository	Fiction plot types	Characters, events, and conflicts	Personal narratives
Hurricane	David Wiesner	✓																				
James and the Giant Peach	Roald Dahl																			✓		
Jumanji	Chris Van Allsburg			✓																		
Just a Dream	Chris Van Allsburg		✓																			
Knots in My Yo-Yo String	Jerry Spinelli																				✓	
Lemony Snicket: The Unauthorized Autobiography	Lemony Snicket												✓									
Let Me Be... the Boss	Brod Bagert									✓												
Lily's Crossing	Patricia Reilly Giff	✓																				
Little House on the Prairie	Laura Ingalls Wilder															✓			✓			
Little Red Riding Hood: A Newfangled Prairie Tale	Lisa Campbell Ernst																					
Loser	Jerry Spinelli								✓													
M is for Magnolia	Michael Shoulders											✓										
Maniac Magee	Jerry Spinelli				✓																	
Matilda	Roald Dahl				✓																	
Mexico City is Muy Grande	Marlene Perez			✓						✓												
Miss Rumphius	Barbara Cooney																			✓		

Index of Literature Models

Title	Author	Dialogue and quotations	Embedded definitions	Exclamations	Simile, metaphor, personification, adjectives, & specificity	Transitions	Pronouns	Dialogue and quotations	Strong verbs, alliteration, and onomatopoeia	Sentence variation	Description	Repetition	Alliteration	Supporting details	Transitions	Endings	Beginnings	Focus & organization in personal narrative	Expository	Fiction plot types	Characters, events, and conflicts	Personal narratives
Monet	Mike Venezia																		✓			
Mother Water, Father Woods	Gary Paulsen																		✓			
Mrs. Katz and Tush	Patricia Polacco										✓											
My Great-Aunt Arizona	Gloria Houston								✓													
Nasty, Stinky Sneakers	Eve Bunting								✓													
Oonawassee Summer	Melissa Forney																	✓				
Owl Moon	Jane Yolen							✓														
Ox Cart Man	Barbara Cooney				✓											✓						
Perfect Pretzels	Marcie Bovetz						✓							✓								
Pierre: A Cautionary Tale in Five Chapters and a Prologue	Maurice Sendak																					
Ramona Quimby, Age 8	Beverly Cleary																			✓		
Ramona's World	Beverly Cleary						✓															
Roll of Thunder, Hear My Cry	Mildred Taylor			✓																		
Sarah, Plain and Tall	Patricia MacLachlan																					
Shoeless Joe and Black Betsy	Phil Bildner						✓										✓					
So You Want to Be President?	Judith St. George																		✓			
Stuart Little	E. B. White																				✓	

Index of Literature Models

Title	Author	Dialogue and quotations	Embedded definitions	Exclamations	Simile, metaphor, personification, adjectives, & specificity	Transitions	Pronouns	Dialogue and quotations	Strong verbs, alliteration, and onomatopoeia	Sentence variation	Description	Repetition	Alliteration	Supporting details	Transitions	Endings	Beginnings	Focus & organization in personal narrative	Expository	Fiction plot types	Characters, events, and conflicts	Personal narratives
Sunflower	David M. Schwartz			✓																		
Tales of a Fourth Grade Nothing	Judy Blume																✓					
Tar Beach	Faith Ringgold				✓																	
The Armadillo from Amarillo	Lynne Cherry													✓								
The Bad Beginning	Lemony Snicket										✓											
The Clown of God	Tomie dePaola									✓												
The Crane's Gift	Steve and Megumi Biddle																✓					
The End	Lemony Snicket															✓						
The Enormous Crocodile	Roald Dahl								✓													
The Ersatz Elevator	by Lemony Snicket							✓														
The Gift	Marcia S. Freeman																		✓			
The Miraculous Journey of Edward Tulane	Kate DiCamillo																			✓		
The Popcorn Book	Tomie dePaola																✓					
The Relatives Came	Cynthia Rylant											✓										
The Slippery Slope	Lemony Snicket												✓									
The Tale of Despereaux	Kate DiCamillo																		✓			
The Trumpet of the Swan	E. B. White		✓																			

Index of Literature Models

Title	Author	Dialogue and quotations	Embedded definitions	Exclamations	Simile, metaphor, personification, adjectives, & specificity	Transitions	Pronouns	Dialogue and quotations	Strong verbs, alliteration, and onomatopoeia	Sentence variation	Description	Repetition	Alliteration	Supporting details	Transitions	Endings	Beginnings	Focus & organization in personal narrative	Expository	Fiction plot types	Characters, events, and conflicts	Personal narratives
The Watsons Go to Birmingham—1963	Christopher Paul Curtis																	✓				
The Wide Window	Lemony Snicket		✓																			
The Winter Room	Gary Paulsen				✓																	
The Wreck of the Zephyr	Chris Van Allsburg	✓																				
Three Days on a River in a Red Canoe	Vera B. Williams																				✓	
Three Names	Patricia MacLachlan		✓																			
Tom	Tomie dePaola							✓														
Twilight Comes Twice	Ralph Fletcher														✓							
Walk Two Moons	Sharon Creech					✓																
What Happens to a Hamburger?	Paul Showers				✓																	
When I Was Little: A Four-Year-Old's Memoir of Her Youth	Jamie Lee Curtis			✓																		
When I Was Young in the Mountains	Cynthia Rylant									✓												
Where the Red Fern Grows	Wilson Rawls				✓																	
Where the Wild Things Are	Maurice Sendak							✓														
Yum! Yuck!	Michaela Morgan			✓																		

Dialogue and quotations

Embedded definitions

Exclamations

Simile, metaphor, personification, adjectives, & specificity

Transitions

Pronouns

Dialogue and quotations

Strong verbs, alliteration, and onomatopoeia

Sentence variation

Description

Repetition

Alliteration

Supporting details

Transitions

Endings

Beginnings

Focus & organization in personal narrative

Expository

Fiction plot types

Characters, events, and conflicts

Personal narratives

Author

Title

Dialogue and quotations													
Embedded definitions													
Exclamations													
Simile, metaphor, personification, adjectives, & specificity													
Transitions													
Pronouns													
Dialogue and quotations													
Strong verbs, alliteration, and onomatopoeia													
Sentence variation													
Description													
Repetition													
Alliteration													
Supporting details													
Transitions													
Endings													
Beginnings													
Focus & organization in personal narrative													
Expository													
Fiction plot types													
Characters, events, and conflicts													
Personal narratives													
Author													
Title													